THE BUDDHA
AND HIS TEACHINGS

THE BUDDHA
AND HIS TEACHINGS

The essential introduction to the origins of Buddhism, from the life of the
Buddha through to the rise of Buddhism as an international religion

A comprehensive overview of the key beliefs and doctrines of the Buddhist
faith, lavishly illustrated with more than 200 photographs and artworks

AUTHOR **HELEN VARLEY** CONSULTANT EDITOR **IAN HARRIS**

southwater

This edition is published by Southwater
an imprint of Anness Publishing Ltd
Blaby Road, Wigston,
Leicestershire LE18 4SE
Email: info@anness.com

www.southwater.com;
www.annesspublishing.com

Anness Publishing has a new picture
agency outlet for images for publishing,
promotions or advertising. Please visit our
website www.practicalpictures.com for
more information.

For Anness Publishing Ltd:
Publisher: Joanna Lorenz
Editorial Director: Helen Sudell
Project Editor: Daniel Hurst
Jacket Designer: Lesley Mitchell
Production Controller: Christine Ni

Produced for Southwater by Toucan Books:
Managing Director: Ellen Dupont
Editor: Anne McDowall
Project Manager: Hannah Bowen
Designer: Elizabeth Healey
Picture Researcher: Tam Church
Proofreader: Marion Dent
Indexer: Michael Dent

ETHICAL TRADING POLICY

At Anness Publishing we believe that
business should be conducted in an ethical
and ecologically sustainable way, with
respect for the environment and a proper
regard to the replacement of the natural
resources we employ. As a publisher, we use a
lot of wood pulp in high-quality paper for
printing, and that wood commonly comes
from spruce trees. We are therefore currently
growing more than 750,000 trees in three
Scottish forest plantations. The forests we
manage contain more than 3.5 times the
number of trees employed each year in
making paper for the books we manufacture.

Because of this ongoing ecological
investment programme, you, as our customer,
can have the pleasure and reassurance of
knowing that a tree is being cultivated on
your behalf to naturally replace the materials
used to make the book you are holding. For
further information about this scheme, go to
www.annesspublishing.com/trees

Previously published as part of a larger volume,
The Illustrated Encyclopedia of Buddhism

PUBLISHER'S NOTE

Although the information in this book is
believed to be accurate and true at the time
of going to press, neither the authors nor the
publisher can accept any legal
responsibility or liability for any errors or
omissions that may have been made.

ACKNOWLEDGEMENTS

The publishers have made every effort to trace the
photograph copyright owners. Anyone we have
failed to reach is invited to contact Toucan Books,
89 Charterhouse Street, London EC1M 6HR, UK.

akg-images /British Library 67b, /Hervé
Champollion 95t, /Jean-Louis Nou 11t, 22t, 26,
60t, 63, 88b, /Gilles Mermet 15t, 35t. **Alamy** /Jim
Allan 86t, Kenneth Garrett/ DanitaDelimont.com
91. **Ancient Art & Architecture Collection**
/C.M. Dixon 18b, 46t, /J.F. Kenney 65t, /T
Paramjit 20b, /Ronald Sheridan 62.
Arkreligion.com /Joan Batten 94b, /Tibor
Bognar 41, 51t, 74b, 83b, 85t, /Dinodia Photo
Library 10b, 29, 70bl, 71b, 73t, 81t, 84t, /Malcolm
Fairman 58b, /Andrew Gasson 35, 88t, /Fiona
Good 47t, /Richard Hammerton 55t, /Nobby
Kealey 56t, /Robin Nichols 78t, /Jan Roberts
72b, /Helene Rogers 19l, 71t, /Jane Sweeney 77t,
93r, /Brian Vikander 42, 64b, 82t, /Maciej
Wojtkowiak 17r, 30t, 39, 79t, 85b, 92t. **The Art
Archive** /Atami Museum Kanagawa/Laurie Platt
Winfrey 40b, /Bibliothèque des Arts Décoratifs,
Paris/Gianni Dagli Orti 36t, /Gianni Dagli Orti
/British Museum 81b, /Stephanie Colasanti 75br,
/Genius of China Exhibition 16bl, /Gianni Dagli
Orti 87t, /Imperial Household Collection
Kyoto/Jobon Rendaiji Temple Kyoto/Laurie Platt
Winfrey 14b, /Koyasan Wakayama
prefecture/Laurie Platt Winfrey 31t /Mohammed
Khalil Museum Cairo /Musée Guimet, Paris
/Alfredo Dagli Orti 15b, /Musée Guimet, Paris
/Gianni Dagli Orti 12t, 31b, 37tl, 50t, 52t, 80t, 89t,
/Museo Nazionale d'Arte Orientale Rome/Gianni
Dagli Orti 18t, /Private Collection Paris/Gianni
Dagli Orti 6, 69, 83t /Sylvan Barnet and William
Burto Collection 38b, 80b, /Mireille Vautier 76t
/Victoria & Albert Museum London/Eileen Tweedy
92br. **The Bridgeman Art Library** 23t, 68t,
70br, 72t, /Bibliothèque Nationale, Paris 48b,
/British Library 13, 32b, /Fitzwilliam Museum,
University of Cambridge 89b, /Paul Freeman 46b,
/Lauros /Giraudon 74b, /National Museum,
Ayutthaya, Thailand 30b, /National Museum of
India 23b, /National Museums of Scotland 34b,
35b, 50b, /Musée Guimet, Paris 11b, 12b, 16br,
/Musée Guimet, Paris/Bonora 14t, /Musée
Guimet, Paris /Giraudon 54, /Musée National de
Phnom Penh, Cambodia/Giraudon 19r, /Museum
of Fine Arts, Boston 34t, /Royal Geographical
Society, London 21. **Corbis** /Dave Bartruff, Inc. 57t,
/Bettmann 16t, /Christophe Boisvieux 52b, 55b,
67t, 82b, /Horace Bristol 74t, /Burstein
Collection/The Munch Museum/The Munch-
Ellingsen Group 40t, /Sheldan Collins 64t, /epa 60b,
/Michele Falzone/JAI 76b, /Michael Freeman 10t,
77br, /Blaine Harrington III 75bl, /Lindsay Hebberd
9, 22b, 45t, /Jon Hicks 25b, 56b, /So Hing-Keung
38t, /Jeremy Horner 53l /Rob Howard 54r, /Lee
Jae-Won/Reuters 61b, /John R. Jones /Papilio 66b,
/Manjunath Kiran/epa 47b, /Charles & Josette
Lenars 17l, /Yang Liu /Craig Lovell 94t, /Diego
Lezama Orezzoli 90t, /Tim Page 73b, /M.A. Pushpa
Kumara/epa 66t, /Phil Schermeister 57b, /Keren Su
90b, /Luca I. Tettoni 20t, 33r, 42t, /Nevada Wier
45b, /Nik Wheeler 95b, /Adam Woolfitt 28, /Alison
Wright 26b, 36b, 53r. **Getty Images** 49t,
/Bavaria/Taxi 48t, /Jan Bruggeman 87t, /Eliot
Elisofon/Time Life Pictures 37tr, /Tony Hallas 37b,
/Hulton Archive 70t, /Liu Jin/AFP 43, /Robert W.
Kelley/Time Life Pictures 32t, /Leelu/Hulton
Archive 27, /Tatyana Makeyeva/AFP 44t, /Hector
Mata/AFP 58t, /National Geographic /Maria
Stenzel 25t, /Christopher Pillitz 92bl, /Robert
Harding 65b, /Robert Harding/Jochen Schlenker
24b, /Robert Nickelsberg/Time Life Pictures 59b,
/Sharon Smith /Photonica 33t, /Tang Chhin
Sothy/AFP 49b /Stone /Hugh Sitton 78b,
/Stone/Pete Turner 86b, /Lakruwan Wanniarachchi
/AFP 44b, /Choi Won-Suk/AFP 77bl. **PA Photos**
/Malcolm Browne 61t, /Misha Japaridze 93l, /David
Longstreath 51b. **Photoshot.com** 8. **Robert
Harding** /Alain Evrard 75t, /Ursula Gahwiler 7b,
/Jochen Schlenker 59t, /Tony Waltham 24t.
shutterstock.com /charles taylor 79b.

CONTENTS

INTRODUCTION

Buddhism is believed to be the world's fifth largest religion today, as ranked by numbers of adherents, and there are also signs that it is one of the fastest-growing religions. Part of Buddhism's appeal is that it has doctrine – a set of principles and beliefs that all practitioners seek to follow – but its teachings are not dogmatic. The Buddha enjoined his followers to question all that he had taught them, so debate is part of Buddhist practice. Further, although he exhorted his followers to go forth and preach the Dharma (his teachings, literally 'the Truth'), Buddhism is not a fervently evangelical faith.

PHILOSOPHY OR RELIGION?

The Buddha did not present himself as the messenger of a supreme God. In fact, Buddhism denies the existence of a creator-god and teaches that no sentient being has a soul, or core identity, that lives on after death. Arguably the oldest and most orthodox of the three main traditions of Buddhism, the Theravada, which claims to follow the Buddha's original teachings, holds that the Buddha was human, not divine. Buddhism has been defined as a 'philosophy and psychology wrapped around a moral code of mind-training'. Many people follow it with the aim of self-transformation, by achieving altered states of consciousness through meditation.

However, Buddhism does not deny the supernatural – the Buddha accepted the existence on Earth of other buddhas before him and of spirit beings, good and evil. Buddhism also has a cosmology. Its universe consists of 31 realms, with hells at the bottom and, above the lower realms inhabited by beings such as animals and humans, a succession of heavens. These hells and heavens are not places of eternal damnation or reward, but temporary staging posts in the cyclical path of birth–death–rebirth.

The concept of 'samsara' – a Sanskrit word that, as it is understood in Buddhism, means not

Left Green Tara, a Buddhist saviour-goddess popular in Tibet, Nepal and Mongolia. She is the feminine counterpart of Avalokiteshvara, the bodhisattva of compassion.

reincarnation, but rebirth or 'rebecoming' – did not originate with the Buddha. It was an idea current in the religions of the 5th century BCE (during the Buddha's lifetime), and one that the Buddha accepted, along with a belief in karma. This is the theory that the balance of good and bad acts committed during a lifetime determines how a being is reborn – in the form of an animal, a human, or a god. These ideas form the core doctrine of Buddhism as a religion.

Mahayana, the second major Buddhist tradition, which emerged in the 1st century BCE, teaches that the Buddha is an earthly manifestation of a celestial buddha. Mahayana schools revere bodhisattvas – semi-divine figures who, through compassion and wisdom, dedicate themselves to the salvation of all sentient beings. Followers of the many Mahayana schools – which include Zen, Nichiren-derived teachings and most other schools popular in the West today – see Buddhism very much as a religion.

Tibetan (Vajrayana or Tantric) Buddhism, a third major tradition, which branched off from the Mahayana during the 1st millennium CE, developed mystic practices as a way of eliminating the fetters that tie beings to samsara. The blend of animism and symbolic Vajrayana ritual practices, employed in Tibetan Buddhism and its various schools and sects, make it fundamentally distinct from the Mahayana and Theravada traditions.

Right Two Japanese Zen monks practise Zazen (seated meditation). Eyes open, they face a blank wall in order to diminish the sensory world. In time, this practice overcomes the mind's defences against total concentration.

Above Thai bhikkhunis carry the Buddha's sacred remains, brought from Sri Lanka during Buddha Day celebrations in Bangkok. This annual festival honours the Buddha's birth, enlightenment and death.

Nevertheless, the goal of all Buddhists is to end the cycle of birth–death–rebirth and to eliminate suffering.

MEDITATION
To meditate is to calm the mind. The Buddha taught that meditation, combined with the observance of a moral code and the development of wisdom, is the path to enlightenment. Through meditation, Buddhists strive to experience what the Buddha experienced – loss of self and ego, the ability to see

things as they really are, and the self-transformation that goes with the attainment of enlightenment. Meditation therefore offers potential for personal growth, spiritual advancement through the conquest of psychological obstacles, and the possibility of greater happiness.

This partly explains the great surge of interest in Buddhism in the Western world in the second half of the 20th century. The image of the Western follower of Buddhism is of a well-educated, often affluent person, who turns to Buddhism in a quest for inner calm.

HOW THIS BOOK IS ORGANIZED
This book begins with the birth of the Buddha and the stories that developed around this exceptional figure. The following chapter delves into the Buddha's teachings and explains the doctrines and concepts that have been central to Buddhism from the very start.

The third chapter discusses the spread of Buddhism over the first centuries after the Buddha passed away, as well as the dissemination of Buddhism across the world, and its transformation as it engaged with new cultures and grew from a minor sect to a major religion.

CHAPTER 1

THE BUDDHA

The historical Buddha, Siddhartha Gautama, was born in India in the 5th century BCE. During the 1st century BCE, the story of his life was written down in the Pali language by monks in Sri Lanka. By that time, the facts of the Buddha's life had been overlaid with folk tales and religious symbolism, so the story that has come down to us contains much myth.

From central India to Central Asia and eastern China, the life of the Buddha is depicted in paintings made by Buddhist monks on the walls of remote caves. As an act of religious merit and to provide teaching aids, they portrayed scenes from the Buddha's life that had been recalled after his death by his disciples. The oldest paintings, at Ajanta in India's Maharashtra province, date from the 2nd century BCE.

Since the 19th century, archaeologists and historians have tried to determine the historical facts behind the story of the Buddha, and they have made many revealing discoveries regarding the origins of Buddhism. However, the 2,500-year-old chronicle of the Buddha's life remains not so much a historical record as an allegory – a story that can be read in many different ways and that is believed by millions of Buddhists to reveal universal truths about the mind, life, death and cosmology.

Opposite A novice Buddhist monk presents an offering of flowers to a Buddha head carved into a tree at Wat Phra Mahathat, Ayutthaya, Thailand. The majority of Thai people are adherents of Buddhism.

Above A scene from the Jataka Tales, a series of stories about the previous life of the Buddha. In this Indonesian relief, Siddhartha Gautama rides in a royal carriage from one palace to another.

THE BUDDHA'S BIRTH

THE BUDDHA WAS BORN IN THE 5TH CENTURY BCE IN THE FAR NORTH OF INDIA (MODERN-DAY NEPAL). THE STORY OF HIS BIRTH HAS BEEN EMBELLISHED BY FOLKLORE AND MYTHOLOGY, AND THERE ARE MANY LEGENDS SURROUNDING HIS CONCEPTION AND BIRTH.

Siddhartha Gautama, who became known as the historical Buddha, was born in what is now southern Nepal in *c.*485BCE. His traditional birth date is earlier – some sources say 624BCE and others 566 or 563BCE – but scholars who have recently studied the chronologies of the Buddha and his contemporaries conclude that if, as the texts state, he lived to the age of 80, he must have died sometime between 410 and 400BCE.

There is little historical evidence for the events of the Buddha's life as recorded in the scriptures. The latter were first written down during the 1st century BCE in Pali, an ancient Indian vernacular, but historians are unable to separate fact from fiction in the stories of the Buddha's life told in either the Pali canon or later Buddhist texts. Over centuries, the accounts were coloured by mythology and laden with symbolism, and different versions of the Buddha's story – all a mixture of scripture, legend and folklore – are told in different places. The story of the Buddha's life, as traditionally recounted, is outlined over the following pages.

THE BUDDHA'S ANCESTRY
Siddhartha Gautama was born into the Shakya clan and is often known as Shakyamuni, 'the sage of the Shakyas'. Although he is said to have been a king's son, the Shakyas were in fact governed not by a monarch but by a small council, perhaps of elders.

Above The Buddha is said to have sprung from Mahamaya's right side, where he was caught in a golden net by mythical beings called *devas*.

The clan belonged to the Kshatriya, or warrior caste, and its territory centred on Kapilavastu on the northern edge of the state of Maghada. Whether or not Siddhartha's family were of royal descent, it is thought that his

EXCAVATING BUDDHA'S BIRTHPLACE
During the 1st millennium CE, pilgrims from countries as distant as China, Tibet, Burma and Indonesia braved sea and mountain crossings to visit Lumbini, birthplace of the Buddha. However, pilgrimages ceased after the 13th-century Muslim conquest of India, when Buddhist sites and monuments were sacked and razed. The site was abandoned and forgotten, and even its name had changed by 1896, when Dr Alois A. Fuehrer, a German archaeologist, discovered an ancient stone pillar inscribed with a homage to the Buddha's birth. The pillar was identified as one erected at Lumbini in the 3rd century BCE by Ashoka, the great Indian emperor of the Mauryan dynasty. The site was excavated and pilgrims flocked to it. In the early 1990s, Japanese archaeologists unearthed a stone slab said to mark the exact spot of the Buddha's birth, and found a bas-relief that portrayed Mahamaya giving birth. In 1997, Lumbini was made a World Heritage Site. Work continues on landscaping and conserving the many ancient buildings and the thousands of artefacts found during excavations.

Left The emperor Ashoka made a pilgrimage to Lumbini in about 250BCE and erected a stone pillar there. Centuries later, lightning broke the pillar in half.

father, who is traditionally called Shuddhodana, and his mother, Mahamaya, may have been nobles, because the records emphasize Shuddhodana's wealth.

BIRTH OF THE BUDDHA

Some versions of the Buddha's birth story claim that he was conceived when his mother dreamt of his descent from heaven in the form of a white elephant. The dream denoted not only the purity of the Buddha's conception, but also that he would become a Universal Monarch – an upright and benevolent world ruler – or a buddha, that is, a spiritually enlightened being. (In Indian mythology, the white elephant was a sign of royal power.)

Ten months later, Mahamaya travelled from Kapilavastu with her retinue of women to give birth at her mother's house in nearby Devadaha, as was the

Right Legend recounts that Mahamaya, the Buddha's mother, conceived during a dream, in which a white, four-tusked elephant penetrated her right side and entered her womb. The dream symbolizes the purity of the Buddha's conception.

custom. On the day of the full moon, the party stopped to rest in a grove of sal trees in the lovely Lumbini Park, where Mahamaya bathed in the Pushkarni Pool. Afterward, catching hold of a sal branch that miraculously swept down within her reach, and facing east, she gave birth.

Many miracles are said to have attended the birth: the newly reborn infant looked in each of the eight cardinal directions, then took seven steps to the east,

Above The Pushkarni Pool, the sacred tank in which Mahamaya is said to have purified herself before giving birth, can still be seen among the ruins at serene Lumbini.

symbolizing the future path of Buddhism, while a lotus flower, signifying enlightenment, sprang up at each of his steps. In a godlike voice, the child is said to have proclaimed, "I am the Leader of the World; I am the Guide of the World. This is my final birth."

EARLY LIFE

NAMED SIDDHARTHA ('HE WHO ATTAINS SUCCESS AND PROSPERITY')
BY HIS FATHER, SIDDHARTHA GAUTAMA IS PORTRAYED AS A
COSSETED AND PROTECTED INFANT, BUT ALSO AS A CHILD WITH
EXTRAORDINARY ABILITIES AND UNUSUAL SENSITIVITIES.

Many tales of the Buddha's birth and early life were recorded in the *Lalitavistara Sutra*, a text believed to have been written around the 3rd century CE, some 700 years after his death.

"Legend is often a poetic form of history, and lifts the story to a plane above the accidents of time and place", wrote Christmas Humphreys, founder of Britain's Buddhist Society, in *Buddhism*, published in 1951. He interpreted the Buddha's life as it is presented in the Pali canon and later scriptures as a hagiography (a religious biographical account), a great symbolic story, like that of Jesus Christ or Moses. He believed that the writers of the scriptures were

Below This ancient stone relief depicts the visit of the sage Ashita to the infant Buddha, and his revelation to his parents, Shuddhodana and Mahayama, that their newborn son would become a great leader.

more concerned with conveying the meaning of the big events in the Buddha's life than their chronological accuracy and that their aim was to relate a wider truth than could be told by an accurate historical record. Thus, everything in the Buddha's life may be read as an allegory – "the mystery story", as Christmas Humphreys put it, "of the evolution of man from birth to final attainment".

CHILDHOOD

Five days after Siddhartha's birth, an ascetic and seer called Ashita came down from his mountain retreat to see the child. Renowned for his supernatural gifts, Ashita had already seen many portents of a great event, such as a vision of gods in the sky, around the tenth month of Mahayama's pregnancy. When he saw Siddhartha's body, the sage recognized all the signs of

Above A Nepalese gilded bronze statue of Mahayama, the moment before she gave birth to the Buddha, dating from the 18th century. Seven days after her delivery she died, symbolizing her purity. The young Siddhartha was cared for by her devoted sister.

a *mahapurusha*, or 'Great Man': the 32 major signs – for example, tightly curled hair circling to the right on his head – and the 80 minor signs. Ashita cried to think that he would be gone when Siddhartha began to reveal his wisdom.

Despite the relative modesty of the Sakka state, the Pali chroniclers emphasize Siddhartha's luxurious upbringing and his education in the 64 spiritual arts, as well as in skills such as archery and horsemanship. They also describe his heroic qualities – how as a youth he defeated all in an archery competition and how, during a ceremony, he fell into a deep meditative trance, although he was untrained in meditation.

The young Siddhartha displayed unusual sensitivities. The scriptures highlight his kindness

to animals and recount an incident when he saved a swan that his cruel cousin Devadatta had shot.

Forewarned by the sage Ashita's prediction that Siddhartha might turn to the *shramana* tradition of wandering ascetics and leave the Shakya clan in search of spiritual enlightenment, his father resolved to protect him against life's uglier realities, such as ageing and decay. The scriptures recount that members of the household who fell ill were kept away from Siddhartha, and that gardeners even removed flowers before they began to wilt.

MARRIAGE

At 16, Siddhartha, now of marriageable age, was presented to eligible young women of his clan and won the hand of the desirable Yashodhara by defeating rival suitors in a contest of strength and martial prowess. Siddhartha married Yashodhara and the couple lived in luxury,

THE SEARCH FOR KAPILAVASTU

After the Buddha's birthplace, Lumbini, was rediscovered in 1896, archaeologists, guided by chronicles written in the 5th and 7th centuries by the Chinese pilgrims Faxian and Xuanzang, identified a site 25km (16 miles) west of the village of Tilaurokot as Kapilavastu, the place where Siddhartha Gautama grew up.

Excavations led by Dr Robin Coningham and Dr Armin Schmidt of the University of Bradford, England, began in 1997, and the team identified moated fortifications, streets and houses, and found jewellery, toys and pottery shards dating from before the 5th century BCE.

Piprawha, a village 93km (58 miles) south of Lumbini in Uttar Pradesh, India, may have been the site of the old Kapilavastu city, before it was moved, or part of Kapilavastu's territory. Excavations of the site by the Archaeological Survey of India during the 1970s located several stupas and a building some believe to be the palace of Shuddhodana. Like many other places associated with the Buddha's life, the site has become a focus of pilgrimage.

moving their household as the seasons changed among three palaces built for them by Shuddhodana in a vast enclosed park on his estates. Yashodhara later gave birth to a son, Rahula. According to some scriptures, Siddhartha had four wives, of whom Yashodhara was the second, and was surrounded by sensual pleasures.

Below Drawing a bow was one of the feats Yashodhara's suitors had to accomplish in order to win her hand in marriage.

THE GREAT DEPARTURE

SUPERNATURAL BEINGS CALLED DEVAS APPEARED AT SPECIAL POINTS
DURING SIDDHARTHA GAUTAMA'S LIFE. IN HIS YOUTH, THEY MADE
HIM AWARE OF HUMAN SUFFERING TO ENSURE THAT HE FULFILLED
HIS DESTINY: TO SEARCH FOR A WAY TO OVERCOME IT.

One day, the Buddha's story continues, Siddhartha was riding in his chariot beyond his father's estate when, approaching the city, he passed an old man shuffling along, bent over a stick, weak and vulnerable. Startled, Siddhartha turned for an explanation to Channa, his charioteer, who told him that the man was aged, and explained that old age, with its infirmities, is the lot of all humanity. Siddhartha returned home, but his thoughts troubled him, preventing him from enjoying the pleasures of his life.

The next day, he drove out again. This time the devas placed in his path a man afflicted with disease. Siddhartha's life had been so sheltered that he knew nothing of illness, but he learned from his charioteer that disease and pain are the burden of humankind. Saddened, he returned home.

Below This illustration from a Chinese sutra (scripture) depicts the Buddha's dissatisfaction with his comfortable life and his decision to leave home to live as an ascetic in the forest.

The following day, Siddhartha set out once more, and at the city gate, he saw a corpse that was being carried to the funeral pyre by grieving mourners. Channa informed him that death is the ultimate, inescapable fate of all living beings.

THE *SHRAMANA*

Distraught, but still wanting to learn about life, Siddhartha made a fourth journey with Channa. This time they passed a poor man who, though he was begging for alms, seemed calm, self-possessed and free from malice. Channa explained that this man was a *shramana*, a wandering ascetic who had renounced the attachments of society and had gone into the world alone to live a homeless existence in search of spiritual fulfilment.

Shuddhodana was anxious that his only son should gain influence in society and become a leader, and he had filled Siddhartha's life with entertainments and other distractions. He also hoped that Siddhartha's newborn son, Rahula

Above Siddhartha Gautama's great encounter with old age, sickness and death showed him that his perception of life had been flawed. His youth, health and happiness would not last, but, inevitably, he would grow old, become ill and die.

(the name means 'tie' or 'impediment'), would bind him to his home and family. However, Siddhartha was deeply impressed by the demeanour of the renunciant he had met and was becoming increasingly disillusioned with his own life of ease.

RENUNCIATION

Among many religious and philosophical trends that arose in India during the 1st millennium BCE was the *shramana* movement. These 'wanderers', many of whom rejected the beliefs of the Brahmans and their rigid adherence to sacrifices described in the Vedas, were forging new beliefs and philosophies. Foremost among them was Mahavira, the reformer of Jainism and a near-contemporary of the Buddha. Many *shramanas* sought to end the cycle of birth-death-rebirth by achieving purity of the soul, or oneness with the Ultimate Reality. *Shramanas* engaged in public debates with orthodox Brahmans and with each other on these issues.

By the 5th century BCE, it had become an established tradition in northern India that, having performed their social duty by marrying and supporting a family, men would renounce family life and caste privileges and seek enlightenment through study and meditation and by living the austere life of a mendicant.

FINAL DEPARTURE

On Siddhartha's 29th birthday, beautiful dancing girls entertained him until he fell asleep. Later that night, he awoke to find that the women asleep around him were no longer so attractive. He was overcome with revulsion at his pointless existence, and his mind filled with thoughts of impermanence, suffering and death.

The idea that a person's soul is reborn after death to live another life was a widely held belief at that time, but to Siddhartha, the prospect of repeated lives and deaths now seemed abhorrent. He therefore resolved to abandon his home and family to search for a way to end this cycle of suffering by living the meditative existence of a *shramana*.

Before leaving, he visited his sleeping wife and son. Resisting the temptation to hold Rahula and awaken them both, he vowed to revisit his son after his enlightenment. He then left his home, riding his horse, Kanthaka, with Channa, his charioteer, clinging to its tail. Devas intervened to silence the sound of the horse's hooves.

Heading south-east, the men reached the River Anoma. There, Siddhartha cut off his hair, exchanged his rich apparel for a mendicant's garb and returned his horse and charioteer to his father as evidence of his renunciation.

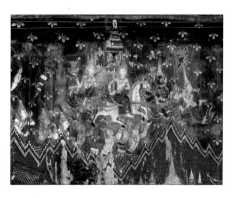

Above Seated on his horse Kanthaka, Gautama Siddhartha takes the first step on his path to enlightenment, as shown in this 19th-century painting of the Great Departure from Wat Ratchasitaram in Thon Buri, Bangkok.

Below By abandoning his fine clothes and jewellery and cutting off his hair, Siddhartha renounced his privileged life and signalled that he would follow the path of an itinerant mendicant.

THE AWAKENING

SIDDHARTHA'S QUEST WAS TO END THE ETERNAL CYCLE OF DEATH–
BIRTH–REBIRTH AND THE SUFFERING OF ALL SENTIENT BEINGS, BUT
HE COULD NOT ACHIEVE ENLIGHTENMENT UNTIL HE HAD FOUND A
MIDDLE WAY BETWEEN HEEDLESS LUXURY AND ASCETIC SELF–DENIAL.

Above Monks, princes and bodhisattvas surround the Buddha as he sits beneath the Bodhi tree in this 2nd-century BCE Kushan stone relief carving in the Indian Museum at Sarnath.

After cutting himself off from his family and making himself homeless, Siddhartha Gautama sought teachers. From the first, he learned the doctrine of the non-existence of all things, and from the second, he learned that there is neither consciousness nor unconsciousness. They taught him techniques such as slow beathing and holding the breath to help control the mind, but these, once learned, did not seem to bring him greater insight. The beliefs of these Brahmans did not resonate with him or help him find his real self. Moreover, he did not manage to conquer his cravings for food, sleep, sensual pleasure and sex.

Siddhartha joined a group of strict ascetics living in the open, quickly adopting a regime of fasting and meditation. He mastered all they knew, and achieved deep trancelike states, but the years of extreme asceticism had weakened him, and by this time he was wasting away. The 32 marks of the 'Great Man', noted at his birth, had disappeared from his body, and he almost died.

THE MIDDLE WAY

Siddhartha decided that asceticism was not the way to enlightenment. As he meditated in a forest beneath a banyan tree, a young mother, Sujata, offered him a bowl of milk rice. Sujata had been visiting the forest in order to supplicate a tree spirit for the gift of a son. Now pregnant, she returned to give thanks with the rice and, mistaking Siddhartha for the tree spirit, she offered it to him. He accepted the gift, and divided it into 49 portions, on which he subsisted for 49 days. His strength returned and, with it, the bodily marks of the great man.

Below Assailed by the demons of Mara, whose name means 'killer', Siddhartha touched the Earth as a testament to his right to enlightenment. The Earth responded with a loud and vigorous tremor.

Left This 6th-century stele from China shows the enlightened Buddha as abhayadana, *the*  *bestower of fearlessness, seated on a lotus, symbol of purification and enlightenment, with his disciples and bodhisattvas.*

Disillusioned at his apparent loss of willpower, five disciples who had joined him went their separate ways and Siddhartha continued alone.

No one existed, Siddhartha realized, who could show him how to achieve enlightenment; he had to find his own way. He understood that this must be a 'middle way' between extremes of self-indulgence and asceticism. Keeping the body strong and healthy was one part of this; so too was cultivating attitudes of mind and behaviour that bring calm.

Working on putting these thoughts into practice, Siddhartha wandered toward the bank of the Niranjana River at Uruvela (now Bodhgaya in Bihar). Aware that the time of his enlightenment was near, he sat, facing east, beneath a pipal (sacred fig) tree, to meditate quietly, vowing to persist until he had attained spiritual awakening.

Below The reliefs at Borobudur in Indonesia tell stories of the Buddha's life from the Lalitavistara. *Here, Siddhartha Gautama bathes in the Niranjana River.*

MARA, 'THE EVIL ONE'

Mara is the name given to the ruler of the World of Desires, governor of the cycle of death and rebirth. Fearful that Siddhartha's enlightenment would illuminate his own shadowy realm, Mara struggled with him beneath the Bodhi tree. First, his demons taunted Siddhartha with fire and darkness, then his three beautiful daughters tried to distract Siddhartha from his meditations. But they failed.

In a final assault, Mara, as Lord of the World, claimed that Siddhartha's seat beneath the Bodhi tree and the gift of enlightenment were his by right. Siddhartha recalled the many compassionate deeds he had performed as proof of his own right to enlightenment. Mara called upon his demons, who shouted their support of their master's claim, then he challenged Siddhartha to find someone to testify to the truth of his words. In response, Siddhartha touched the Earth with his right hand, supplicating it to bear witness to his past acts of compassion.

ENLIGHTENMENT

As he meditated, he was attacked by the powers of Mara, the tempter, the deva or spirit associated with death and rebirth. Mara represents the forces of the mind that militate against liberation and enlightenment. Siddhartha refused to be disturbed by Mara's barbs, which turned to flowers in the face of his calm.

The Awakening took place in three phases. First, Siddhartha fell into progressively deeper stages of meditation; then he recalled his past lives and saw the past lives of others. Finally, he understood the Dharma, or law, the causes and effects that keep the cycle of death and rebirth in motion. From this point on, he was called the Buddha, 'the Awakened One'.

Below Sujata offered the meditating Siddhartha Gautama milk rice in a golden bowl. Since a monk may not keep any precious object, he threw the bowl into a river.

TURNING THE WHEEL OF THE DHARMA

THE SCRIPTURES MAKE CLEAR THAT THE BUDDHA, HAVING ATTAINED ENLIGHTENMENT, COULD HAVE LEFT THE WORLD FOREVER. INSTEAD, HE CHOSE TO REMAIN INCARNATE, IN ORDER TO TEACH THE LAW HE HAD DISCOVERED TO THOSE WHO WERE READY TO LISTEN.

Above This 7th-century Tibetan mural shows the Buddha 'setting the Wheel of the Dharma in motion' by giving his First Sermon in the Deer Park at Isipatana, modern Sarnath.

After his awakening, the Buddha sat cross-legged in meditation beneath the pipal tree (the 'Bodhi' or 'Enlightenment' tree) at Uruvela for seven days. He then remained close to the tree for seven weeks as he contemplated his experience of enlightenment. During the third week, he walked up and down as he meditated. Today, stones at the Bodhgaya temple mark his footsteps.

During the fifth week, the Buddha turned his attention to the task of teaching the doctrine that had just been revealed to him. He had doubts about how successful he could be: "The truth remains hidden from him who is in the bondage of hate and desire," he mused. "Nirvana remains incomprehensible and mysterious to the vulgar, whose minds are beclouded with worldly interests. Should I preach the doctrine and mankind not comprehend it, it would bring me only fatigue and trouble." He was in half a mind to end his sojourn on Earth.

At this point, a deity, Brahma Sahampati, appeared to the Buddha and urged him to teach. He received a vision of lotus flowers, some blooming above the water, others in bud, and some too far beneath the surface to flower. He realized that they were like people, and decided that those in the middle group – *shramanas* already on the path to enlightenment – would be most receptive to his message.

He ate his first meal since Sujata's offering of milk rice during the seventh week, when two foreign merchants approached and offered him food, a sign that the

Left The Buddha eats a meal after his awakening, from a bowl miraculously fashioned from four bowls of precious metals, presented to him by the guardian gods of each of the cardinal points.

Buddha had returned to human existence. He imparted his message to them, and the two men became his first lay followers.

THE SERMON IN THE DEER PARK

His 'divine eye' told the Buddha that the two *shramanas* who had taught him to meditate had died. But he also perceived that the five disciples who had separated themselves from him when he gave up the ascetic life were now in Isipatana (modern Sarnath, near the holy city of Varanasi). Having found them there, he instructed them that they must now call him 'Tathagata', a form of address reserved for those who have travelled the path to enlightenment.

The Buddha made this meeting the occasion for setting in motion the Wheel of the Dharma (his teaching of the law, or doctrine) by giving his first sermon in the Deer Park at Isipatana on the evening of the full moon in June/July.

He began by explaining why he had abandoned extreme asceticism, and how the path to enlightenment lies along the Middle Way. In conclusion, he elucidated the doctrine he had understood as a result of his enlightenment, beginning with the Four Noble Truths.

THE COMMUNITY

The five men, with their disciplined minds and bodies, were quickly able to understand the Buddha's explanation of the nature of reality and the truth. Five days later, he gave another sermon, this time on impermanence and the idea of the 'non-self'. One man rapidly attained enlightenment and the others soon followed. They became the first members of the first Buddhist Sangha, or monastic community.

THE DEER PARK AT SARNATH

The peaceful Deer Park at Isipatana, called Sarnath today, where the Buddha first taught and transmitted the Dharma and where the first Sangha (monastic community) was founded, became a sacred place of pilgrimage after his death. Stupas, shrines, viharas (monasteries) and temples were built. The Mauryan emperor Ashoka made a pilgrimage there during the 3rd century BCE, and erected a stupa to mark the spot where the Buddha is said to have given his first sermon, and a stone pillar with an inscription. During the Gupta empire, 4th–6th century CE, Ashoka's stupa, known as the Dhamekh stupa, which had by then been rebuilt and enlarged, was faced in beautifully carved stone, some sections of which survive.

During the 12th century, Turkish Muslims sacked and looted Isipatana and killed its monks. The site was later raided for building stone. It was revitalized after 19th-century archaeologists excavated an ancient brick stupa, dating from before the 3rd century BCE, ancient inscriptions, and a stone casket containing relics and precious stones. Later excavations revealed a vihara, a temple, with a magnificent large frieze, and hundreds of exquisite statues of the Buddha.

Below Sarnath is a peaceful spot full of stupas and other remains from the time of the Buddha. This photograph shows the main shrine at the site.

Above Meditating beside Muchalinda Lake six weeks after his enlightenment, the Buddha was sheltered from a storm by the Muchalinda, a naga, or snake spirit, which coiled around him.

THE BUDDHA'S TEACHINGS

FOR MORE THAN 40 YEARS, THE BUDDHA AND HIS FOLLOWERS TRAVELLED THROUGHOUT EASTERN AND NORTHERN INDIA, SPEAKING TO THE PEOPLE AND INSTRUCTING NEW CONVERTS IN THE PATH TO ENLIGHTENMENT. HE ALSO PERFORMED MANY MIRACLES.

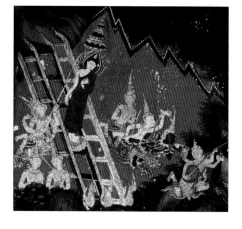

Above One year, the Buddha secretly ascended into the Heaven of the Thirty-three. There he found the reborn spirit of his dead mother. He stayed through a rainy season, teaching her, before descending a ladder to his followers waiting on Earth.

From a nucleus of six, the community that had formed around the Buddha at Isipatana (now Sarnath) quickly grew into a movement. One young convert was Yashas, a youth who, like Siddhartha Gautama years earlier, had realized the pointlessness of his comfortable existence. Yashas became the first lay person to join the Sangha and he went on to achieve enlightenment.

Yashas' father, likewise, became a lay follower, while his mother was the first female disciple. News of Yashas' enlightenment spread quickly, and more than 50 of the family's friends and acquaintances approached the Sangha and were eventually ordained. From

Below A 3rd-century Indian relief of the Buddha preaching, with women on the left and disciples in a seated meditation pose on the right.

this nucleus of adherents, the Buddha sent forth 60 to spread his teachings.

ON THE MOVE

The Sangha remained in Isipatana during the rainy season, when movement was difficult, then resumed the peripatetic life of a *shramana* group.

At Uruvela (now Bodhgaya), the Buddha approached a group of ascetics, the Kashyapa brothers and their more than 1,000 disciples, who were fire-worshippers. He persuaded their leader that fire-worship impeded their search for enlightenment because it did not free them from ignorance, craving and hatred. The brothers received his teaching and became converts.

Within a year of his awakening, the Buddha, accompanied by many monks, returned to his former home at Kapilavastu. Although his

family were initially shocked at his austere way of life, most of them eventually converted to his path. Many of the Shakya clan also became his followers.

The doctrine propounded by the Buddha was not restricted to people of particular classes or castes, unlike the religion of the Brahmans and others who followed the *Upanishads*. He shared the Dharma with all, from the barber Upali of the Sudra, or servant caste, to King Bimbisara of Rajagriha (modern Rajgir, Bihar) and his court. The Buddha's name spread, and many came to hear him preach.

THE FIRST MONASTERY

Followers of other religions and teachers sought out the Sangha while the monks rested in the Veluvana Bamboo Grove at Rajagriha, which had been given to them by King Bimbisara. Many of these *shramanas* were dissuaded from their extreme asceticism and were ordained.

Some time later, a rich merchant and convert, Anathapindika, invited the Buddha to his home

Left The Buddha spent long hours in meditation before he achieved enlightenment. This Tibetan thangka (painted or embroidered banner) shows him meditating with Mañjushri, the Bodhisattva of Wisdom, and Vajrapani, the Buddha's protector and guide.

SANSKRIT TERMS

arhat worthy one; a Buddhist or Jain who has gained insight into the true nature of existence and will not be reborn.
bhikkhu a fully ordained Buddhist monk. Nuns are bhikkhunis. (In Sanskrit, the corresponding terms are *bhikshu* and *bhikshuni*.)
Dharma the universal law, or truth, as proclaimed by the Buddha.
Sangha a Buddhist Order, or monastic community.
shramana a religious seeker; a person who avidly pursues spiritual knowledge, usually as a mendicant and homeless wanderer.
Tathagata the name the Buddha Shakyamuni used when referring to himself. The word literally means 'one who has thus come'.

at Shravasti, capital of Kosala, a *mahajanapada* bordering Maghada. A vihara (monastery) called Jetavana was founded there.

Jetavana became the home of the Sangha, and the Buddha gave most of his sermons and discourses there. The Buddha used his experience, gathered over several lifetimes, and his penetrating insight to make his teaching exactly suited to his students' capacities to understand the Dharma. His success was spectacular, since many travelled the path of enlightenment and became arhats. In time, Jetavana would also become the Buddha's final resting place.

GREAT MAGICAL WONDERS

The impact of the Buddha's teachings and his growing following aroused jealousy among other religious teachers. During the sixth year after his enlightenment, he was challenged by six leaders of other sects to a public debate in Shravasti. He announced that he would defeat them in the shade of a mango tree. He arrived to find all the mango trees cut down, but he cast a mango seed on the ground and a tree sprouted and grew tall.

The Buddha defeated the arguments of the teachers and made converts of them, then he performed 'twin miracles', making fire and water shoot out from his body. Finally, the Buddha projected simultaneous images of himself in four different postures. These and many other miraculous events in the Buddha's life became popular themes of Buddhist art in later centuries.

THE BUDDHA'S PASSING

IN HIS EIGHTIES, AND APPROACHING THE END OF HIS HUMAN LIFE, THE BUDDHA ENTERED A GROVE OF SAL TREES. THERE, SURROUNDED BY HIS DEVOTED MONKS, HE ACHIEVED PARINIRVANA – THE STATE OF ULTIMATE PEACE THAT FOLLOWS THE DEATH OF A BUDDHA.

Above Devadatta made three attempts on the Buddha's life: he sent assassins to kill him, then pushed a boulder over a cliff as the Buddha walked below. Finally, he set a raging elephant in his path, but, as shown here, the Buddha pacified the beast with his kindness.

The ancient texts tell few stories about the Buddha's last years, but the Pali *Maha-parinibbana Sutta*, or 'Sermon of the Great Passing', recounts in some detail the events of his last three months. Tradition says that the Buddha lived until he was 80, and by then his sect, although still small and scarcely known outside northern India, was established and respected for its doctrine of compassion and its strict precepts.

ATTACKS ON THE BUDDHA

The Buddha was challenged on several occasions during his later years, not only by the leaders of rival sects, but also by two beings, who, some commentators have theorized, symbolize the dark elements of the psyche that militate against change, success and liberation. One was Devadatta, the Buddha's cousin, who was ordained a monk but is portrayed as consumed with egotism and jealousy. One text tells how he tried, unsuccessfully, to take over the Sangha. Overcome with hatred and rivalry, he made three attempts to kill the Buddha. Finally, he caused a split among the monks.

Mara, 'the Evil One', had attacked Siddhartha during his spiritual awakening and tried to dissuade him from taking the gift of the Dharma to the people. As the Buddha approached the last months of his life, Mara appeared to him again, tempting him to free himself from human pain, to enter nirvana there and then. Until his task was complete, the Buddha replied, he would not seek release.

THE DEATH OF THE BUDDHA

During his final year, the Buddha travelled with Ananda, one of his chief disciples, who was his cousin and personal attendant of 25 years, through the northern states. In Maghada, he experienced a brief illness. Afterward, Ananda asked who would lead the Sangha when he had gone. The Sangha needs no central authority but the Dharma, was the reply, "...be ye islands unto yourselves....Hold fast to the Dharma as an island.... Look not for refuge to anyone besides yourselves...."

At Vaishali (near Pataliputra, modern Patna), the Buddha made his final address to his disciples. He urged them not to take his teachings on trust but rather to gain their knowledge directly, by experiencing the truth of them personally through meditation. He also appealed to them not to keep the joy of enlightenment to themselves, but to share it with the world.

Left The Buddha lay down on his right side between two sal trees, with his head facing the north, and withdrew into a meditative trance. Sacred texts state that at the moment of his passing, a violent tremor shook the Earth.

Right The young monks who were still searching for liberation and enlightenment expressed grief at the Buddha's passing, and at the loss of his guidance and teaching.

Travelling on, he stopped to dine with Cunda, a blacksmith, who prepared a special dish that is said to have contained pork. Afterward, the party continued northward and came to a grove of sal trees near Kushinara. The Buddha, ill with dysentery, caused, perhaps, by his last meal, lay down among the trees.

During his last hours, the Buddha asked his disciples whether they had any doubts about the Dharma. None did. He reassured the weeping Ananda that he would soon experience enlightenment. Then he uttered his final words, "Decay is inherent in all component things! Work out your own salvation with diligence."

Finally, he entered the highest states of consciousness and passed into parinirvana – the final nirvana of one who has experienced enlightenment, the final release from the cycle of rebirth.

BUDDHAS PAST AND FUTURE

'Tathagata', which means 'one who has thus come' or 'one who has thus gone', expresses the belief that Buddha Shakyamuni (the name given to Siddhartha Gautama) was the 25th in a line of buddhas, each of whom had resided on Earth for one historical cycle to teach the Dharma. The Jataka Tales are stories about the Buddha's previous lives. In one, Buddha Shakyamuni describes his encounter with Buddha Dipankara, whose admirable qualities so impressed him that he decided to cultivate them in himself.

When the current historical era has ended, Buddhists believe that a new buddha will be born, attain enlightenment, teach the Dharma and live a human life. That buddha is the Bodhisattva Natha (meaning 'Protector'), who will be born as the Bodhisattva Maitreya. Future buddhas reside in the Tushita heaven, one of many heavens in Buddhist teaching. In China, over the last two millennia, many individuals have declared themselves to be the Bodhisattva Maitreya, and their claims and cults have sparked political rebellions.

Right According to Buddhist teachings, the Bodhisattva Maitreya, depicted in this 2nd-century BCE sculpture, will succeed the Buddha Shakyamuni as the next buddha. He is an enlightened being who will, in a future age, come to Earth to teach the Dharma.

STUPAS

THE BUILDINGS MOST CLOSELY ASSOCIATED WITH BUDDHISM, STUPAS ARE SHRINES ORIGINALLY BUILT TO HOUSE RELICS OF THE BUDDHA, AND ARE SYMBOLS OF HIS MIND AND THE PATH TO ENLIGHTENMENT. MANY ARE EXPRESSIONS OF THE FINEST ARCHITECTURE AND ART.

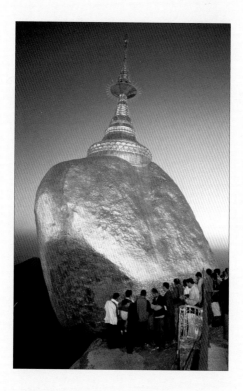

Before his death, the Buddha gave instructions for his funeral. His body was to be accorded the honours of a world ruler – washed, embalmed and carried in a coffin to the funeral pyre, and his ashes were to be buried in a stupa (a burial mound) at a crossroads.

With all the respect due to the ruler who brought the Dharma to the world, the funeral rites were carried out according to his wishes by the princes of Malla, the *mahajanapada,* where the Buddha died, and were accompanied by processions, music and dancing.

Disputes broke out among neighbouring rulers as to where the Buddha's ashes should rest.

Below These chortens (stupas) were erected in the mountains of Ladakh above the 17th-century Hemis gompa, *the largest and wealthiest monastery in Ladakh.*

To avoid conflict, they were divided among eight claimants. Each one erected a stupa over the relics given, and these stupas were venerated by the Buddha's followers.

THE FIRST STUPAS

Stupas did not originate with the Buddha, however. Archaeology has shown that from early Vedic times in India, the dead were cremated and their incinerated remains buried with ceremony in a funerary mound, known as a stupa.

The Buddha's wishes to be buried as a *chakravartin*, or world ruler, recall the tumuli at Lauriya Nandangarh, Bihar, dating from the 700s BCE. These grave mounds are so large that they are thought to belong to kings. Archaeologists believe that a wooden post at the apex of the dome may have supported a parasol, which was seen as a symbol of royal authority.

Above A hair of the Buddha is said to lie beneath this rock, which forms part of the Kyaiktiyo stupa in Burma. Pilgrims have covered it in gold leaf.

Buddhist stupas, built in brick and stone, have a cupola – representing the dome of heaven – which rests on a cylindrical base. Rising from the centre of the dome (or *anda*, literally 'egg', signifying the cycle of rebirth) is a *harmika* (platform), sheltered by a *chattra* (parasol), the two denoting enlightenment. Stupa architecture embodies many layers of complex Buddhist religious symbolism, so a stupa becomes a meditative focus for adherents walking the circumambulatory path around it.

Stupas are believed to radiate a beneficial influence over their locality, and they attract pilgrims. During the 3rd century BCE, the emperor Ashoka, a Buddhist convert, is said to have collected the Buddha's relics from seven of the eight original stupas, divided them into 84,000 portions, and vowed to send each portion to a different part of his empire and erect a stupa there. He had stupas erected all

Left The Buddha's all-seeing eyes gaze in all directions across the Kathmandu Valley in Nepal from the gilded and whitewashed Swayambhunath stupa. This stupa is said to have been built on the spot where a miraculous lotus was planted by an antecedent of the Buddha Shakyamuni. Between the eyes is the Sanskrit number one, symbolizing the single Buddhist path to enlightenment, and above it is the third eye, signifying wisdom.

Below The parasol of the 12th-century Kiri (White) vihara soars above the ancient city of Polonnaruwa, Sri Lanka's former capital. Its unrestored whitewashed plaster survived seven centuries of abandonment after the collapse of the Polonnaruwa kingdom.

over India and they became centres of pilgrimage and veneration. Large numbers were destroyed by later Hindu and Islamic dynasties, but many remain.

ARTISTIC TRADITIONS

Many early stupas are unadorned, but beautiful decoration, in the form of reliefs, sculpture, inscriptions, paintings and *torana*, or entrance gates, is a feature of later buildings. Artists expressed the architectural, artistic and folk traditions they knew in these religious structures. Thus, stupas contributed to the artistic development of many Asian countries where Buddhism spread and evolved. In Sri Lanka, the Himalayan kingdoms, and the countries of Central, East and South-east Asia, the stupa took on new architectural forms and different symbolism. 'Stupa' is a Sanskrit word. In Sri Lanka, it is called a dagoba, in Tibet a chorten, and in Thailand a chedi.

From the Buddha's time, stupas have been built to enshrine the relics of respected monks and teachers; over the last century, some have also been erected in the West.

BUDDHIST PILGRIMAGES

IN THE BUDDHA'S LAST DISCOURSE BEFORE HIS DEATH, HE URGED HIS FOLLOWERS TO MAKE PILGRIMAGES TO THE PLACES OF HIS BIRTH, ENLIGHTENMENT, FIRST SERMON AND DEATH. TO THESE FOUR HOLY SITES, BUDDHISTS LATER ADDED FOUR MORE 'GREAT PLACES'.

Pilgrimage has had a significant place in the practice of Buddhism since at least the 3rd century BCE, when Ashoka the Great visited the Buddhist holy sites that lay within his empire. From ancient times, Buddhists visited the 'Eight Great Places' included in the texts and commentaries. After the 12th century, with the demise of Buddhism in India, many of the sacred sites were destroyed and subsequently forgotten. However, as Buddhism spread, new pilgrimage sites were established outside India: for example, the Chinese mountain monastery of Wutai Shan in north-eastern Shanxi province, where Mañjushri, Bodhisattva of Wisdom, resided.

From the 5th century CE, Chinese and, later, Tibetan pilgrims set out on long and dangerous journeys to India in search of Buddhist scriptures. Their accounts are a unique record of Buddhism and sacred sites in India during these centuries.

EIGHT GREAT PLACES

Traditionally, 'Eight Great Places' are visited by Buddhist pilgrims. The first four are major sites associated with key events in the Buddha's life; the others are sites of miraculous events.

- **Lumbini**, Nepal. The Buddha's birthplace.
- **Uruvela** (now Bodhgaya), Bihar, India. The place where the Buddha attained enlightenment.
- **Isipatana** (modern Sarnath, near Varanasi, India). The Buddha preached his first sermon, so turning the Wheel of the Dharma, in the Deer Park here.
- **Kushinara** (modern Kushinagar). The place where the Buddha passed away and entered nirvana.
- **Shravasti** (in north-eastern Uttar Pradesh). The Buddha

Above Rajagriha (modern Rajgir) was the capital of the kingdom of Maghada during the time of the Buddha, who preached many important sermons there.

performed 'Twin Miracles' here, sending fire and water from his body and appearing in several places at once. The remains of the Jetavana, the first Buddhist vihara, are here.
- **Rajagriha** (modern Rajgir, near Bihar). The Veluvana Bamboo Grove at Rajagriha was a retreat for the Sangha, a gift from King Bimbisara. A vihara was built and the Buddha delivered important sermons here.
- **Sankashya** (modern Sankissa). The Buddha ascended to the Tushita heaven, where his mother had been reborn as a male god. Following in the tradition of his predecessors, the Buddha taught the Dharma to his mother before descending to Earth at Sankashya.
- **Nalanda** (near Bihar). The Buddha preached for long periods at a mango grove here, where a tree miraculously grew from a toothpick he discarded. It became renowned as a great Buddhist centre of teaching.

Left Monks circumambulate the excavated remains of stupas and other ancient buildings at Lumbini, Nepal, the birthplace of the Buddha.

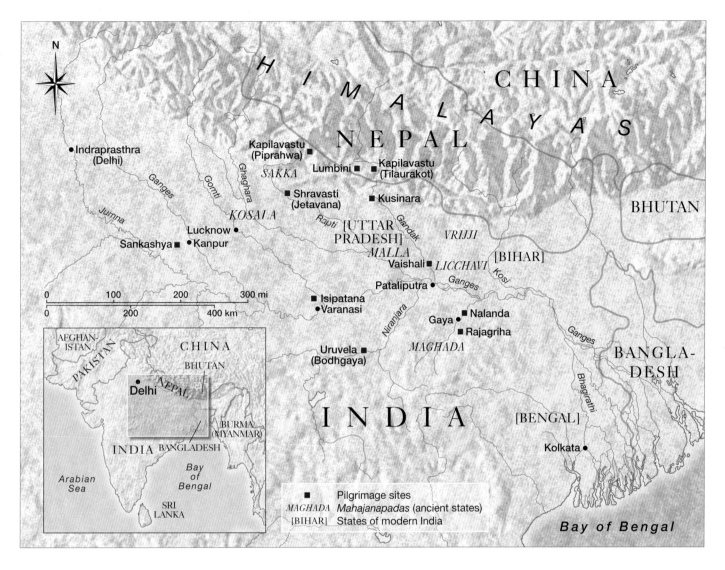

OTHER PILGRIMAGE SITES

Many other places in north–eastern India were visited by the Buddha and number among the holy places, including the sacred Hindu city of Varanasi (Benares). Other places have become pilgrimage sites in modern times, including the excavations at Kapilavastu (at Tilaurakot, Nepal, and Piprawha, Uttar Pradesh, India), the city where the Buddha grew up, and Vaishali (Bihar), where the Buddha miraculously cured a pestilence that was attacking the city's inhabitants. This was also the last place he visited before his death.

Right Sarnath, where the Buddha preached many sermons, was once the site of many monasteries, temples and stupas. It is still a sacred pilgrimage site.

NORTHERN INDIA AT THE TIME OF THE BUDDHA

The map above shows the mahajanapadas, *or city-states, of northern India during the 5th century* BCE, *and the principal sites associated with the Buddha's life. Today these places have become major pilgrimage sites for Buddhists.*

CHAPTER 2

WHAT THE BUDDHA TAUGHT

Siddhartha Gautama is believed to have achieved enlightenment by the age of about 30. Then, as the Buddha, he gathered a group of followers and travelled around northern India, teaching all who came to hear him, as well as debating with Brahmans, Jains and followers of other religions and belief systems. His teachings and discourses, as recalled by his disciples, were preserved by them after his death as the doctrine of the religion that later came to be called Buddhism.

Just eight weeks after his enlightenment, the Buddha delivered his key message to a group of ascetics, his former companions in his quest for spiritual awakening, in a deer park near Varanasi. That message, though profound, may be summarized in four simple statements – the 'Four Noble Truths' about the nature of reality – which form the foundation of Buddhist doctrine. In the fourth of these, the Buddha provides a way of ending repeated cycles of birth, death and rebirth – his 'Noble Eightfold Path' – which can lead to self-transformation and enlightenment. The Noble Eightfold Path provides guidelines for the practice of morality, mental training (or meditation) and insight – the three indispensable elements in the enlightenment process.

Opposite The spoked wheel, or Dharmachakra, *an ancient symbol of sovereignty and the law in Indian art, has been a symbol of the Buddha's teachings, or Dharma, since the early centuries BCE.*

Above Scriptures written in Sanskrit helped preserve the teachings of not only Buddhism but also Hinduism and Jainism. Some Sanskrit terms are common to all three religions, but the concepts ascribed to them vary.

THE DISCIPLES

SHORTLY AFTER THE BUDDHA'S DEATH 500 ARHATS CONVENED A COUNCIL IN A CAVE OUTSIDE RAJAGRIHA, CAPITAL OF THE HEARTLAND OF BUDDHISM, MAGHADA. THEIR MISSION WAS TO FIND A WAY OF PRESERVING THE BUDDHA'S TEACHINGS.

The Buddha's disciples were a loosely organized network of groups who lived in small communities or travelled across the Gangetic Plain, discussing and teaching the Dharma and practising meditation. During the rainy season, these groups converged at Jetavana or another of the retreats lay followers had donated to the Sangha for a few weeks of spiritual renewal. Their focus had been on the Buddha, and, obedient to his revelation that there should be no central authority but the Dharma, the disciples appointed no successor after his death. When the duties connected with the division and preservation of his relics were over, they drifted away from Kushinara, the place of his passing into parinirvana.

Above Mahakashyapa, like Siddhartha Gautama , had abandoned the life of a wealthy Brahman for an austere existence. He remained an ascetic even after accepting the teaching of the Buddha and attaining enlightenment.

THE FIRST BUDDHIST COUNCIL

Under the Buddha's inspiring guidance, many of his disciples had themselves achieved enlightenment. After his passing, these arhats preoccupied themselves with the question of how to preserve his teachings – his words as they had heard and remembered them – for future generations. They also realized the need to codify the rules of the Sangha in order to prevent any group from straying too far from the central core of the Dharma.

Within about a year of the Buddha's parinirvana, therefore, they decided to hold a meeting. According to tradition, 500 arhats assembled in a cave at Rajagriha, Maghada's capital, to review all of the Buddha's teachings. Perhaps by common consent, Mahakashyapa, an honoured elder of the Sangha who had assisted the Buddha, led the First Buddhist Council.

The Buddha had the gift of teaching according to the abilities and understanding of the listener or group to whom he was speaking. He would give examples, tell stories and put things in ways his listeners would understand. This meant that no one person had ever heard everything he had taught. Writing was a specialized skill in India in the 4th century BCE, and most Sangha members were probably illiterate, so nothing was written down. Mahakashyapa's plan was to ask each of the 500 arhats to repeat from memory the Buddha's teachings they knew.

THE BUDDHIST CANON

Ananda was asked to recount each of the Buddha's discourses he had personally heard. He began by saying where each discourse had taken place, then he repeated what he had heard the Buddha say. Others who had also been present verified or disputed Ananda's memory and a version was agreed.

Another of the disciples, Upali, who had formerly been a low-caste barber, recited the 227 rules that he recalled the Buddha imposing on the community

Above Two leading disciples – Sariputra, renowned for his wisdom, and Maudgalyayana, famous for mind-reading and other supernatural skills – stand on either side of the Buddha in this Thai painted silk banner.

Right Younger monks grieved at the Buddha's passing into parinirvana, as depicted in this 11th-century Japanese painting on silk. But the arhats reflected serenely on his liberation from the cycle of death and rebirth.

whenever he rebuked a monk for doing something that might harm someone or discredit the Sangha, or that did not fit the spirit of the Dharma.

Finally, Mahakashyapa repeated the Buddha's analyses of philosophy and metaphysics – how the human mind works, for instance, and the mechanisms that give rise to the cycle of death and rebirth.

Mahakashyapa then divided the assembly into three groups and charged each with memorizing one category of teachings. These later came to be called *Pitaka*, meaning 'baskets' or 'collections'. The teachings recited by Mahakashyapa, for example, were called the *Abhidharma Pitaka*, meaning 'The Basket of Higher Knowledge'.

The Saptaparni cave, the place where the Sangha held the First Buddhist Council, is among the many sites in Rajagriha (now Rajgir) that are today visited by Buddhist pilgrims.

THE DISCIPLE ANANDA

As the Buddha's personal attendant for many years, Ananda had heard more of the Buddha's teachings than anyone, so his presence was needed at the First Buddhist Council. However, only arhats could attend, and he had not attained enlightenment. It is written that Mahakashyapa pressed Ananda to practise meditation intensively to achieve enlightenment – and also that he charged him with having committed a disastrous misjudgement shortly before the Buddha's final illness. On the road to Vaishali, the Buddha may have suggested that Ananda could ask him to prolong his earthly existence until the end of the current era, more than two centuries hence. Perhaps because he did not grasp the significance of the Buddha's words, Ananda did not respond. Thereupon, the Buddha 'rejected his vital constituents'. As if to confirm his action, the Earth shook. Ananda, in crisis, threw himself into meditation and, it is recorded, successfully achieved enlightenment on the night that the Council opened.

Right The disciple Ananda, shown in this 6th-century marble sculpture from China, was the Buddha's cousin and his attendant for 25 years. He heard more of the Buddha's teachings than any other disciple and was famous for his ability to memorize.

31

THE DHARMA

IN HIS TEACHINGS, THE BUDDHA EXPLAINED HIS OWN INTERPRETATION OF THE DHARMA – THE LAW THAT GOVERNS THE UNIVERSE. HE SPOKE OF IMPERMANENCE, DEATH AND REBIRTH AND REVEALED THE PATH TO LIBERATION FROM THE TORMENTS OF EARTHLY LIFE.

Above The palm of this Siamese Hand of the Buddha is inscribed with the Wheel of the Dharma. The finger and thumb form a circle in the teaching sign, or vitarka *mudra.*

Although it is a central part of Buddhism, the concept of Dharma existed long before the Buddha. The term derives from a Sanskrit word meaning 'to sustain' or 'uphold', and it appeared in the Vedas on law and customs. The Hindus interpreted Dharma as the law of the cosmos, which governs religious, social and individual action, and the Jains conceived of it as the life-force and as virtue.

The Dharma taught by the Buddha Shakyamuni (known as the Buddha-Dharma) includes many beliefs that were popular in 5th-century BCE India. For example, the Buddha accepted the Brahmanical pantheon of gods, devas and other supernatural entities, and their role became increasingly important as Buddhism spread across the East. The Buddha was also influenced by the Hindu belief in samsara, or reincarnation. Upon his enlightenment, he remembered his many previous lives and recalled that he was 24th in a line of buddhas, each of whom had been reborn for the purpose of teaching the Dharma. Over millions of years, knowledge of the Dharma faded, and the task of each buddha had been to teach it anew. The Buddha Shakyamuni fulfilled this task as much by example as by teaching. The very pattern of his life – renunciation, meditation and enlightenment – is also the Dharma, or spiritual truth, of earthly human existence.

SELF AND SOUL

The Buddha's unique contribution to Indian philosophy was an alternative to belief in a human soul. Central to Brahmanism was the idea that every living being has an eternal spiritual life-force, or soul, that survives unchanged after death and is reborn. This personal soul, called the *atman*, is part of a universal soul, called Brahma.

The Buddha searched but could find no evidence for the existence of a creator god or an eternal soul. He conceived of the

Left A Jain diagram of the universe. Jainism, established in the 7th–5th centuries BCE, shares many concepts with Buddhism, such as the idea of continual rebirth until the soul can achieve true liberation from the body.

components of all five aggregates change. Thus, although everyone has a personality, or self, there is no core, unchanging self, or immortal soul. *Anatman* is the Sanskrit term for the Buddhist idea of 'non-self'; it is *anatta* in Pali.

Throughout the course of their lives, individuals commit good and bad actions, and in so doing, they forge a moral identity, which, the Buddha taught, survives death and is reborn. He encapsulated this in his teachings on the Four Noble Truths.

Below A standing or walking buddha making the double abhaya *mudra usually signifies 'preaching'. The* abhaya *mudra – right hand raised, palm facing outward – is the gesture of friendship and protection.*

Above The hands of this statue of the Buddha are in the Dharmachakra *mudra, or gesture, signifying that the Buddha is 'Turning the Wheel of the Dharma', or preaching the First Sermon in the Deer Park at Sarnath.*

(called *rupa*); feelings, such as pleasure and pain (*vedana*); all that can be perceived and imagined (*samjna*); character traits and motivating forces, such as desire (*samskara*); and consciousness or mind (*vijñana*).

None of these aggregates is permanent, and while all are part of the 'self', none is, or becomes, the soul. Although the body is part of the self, the self is more than the body's shape or how it functions, and the body changes as a person ages. In fact, all through life, the

world and everything in it – trees, water, people – as made up of components or qualities such as colour, sight or youth. Humans are composed of five groups or aggregates of components, known as skandhas: the physical body

THE BUDDHIST UNIVERSE

UNENLIGHTENED BEINGS INHABIT THREE SPHERES OF EXISTENCE IN THE BUDDHIST UNIVERSE, WHERE THEY DWELL IN SEPARATE REALMS. THE KARMA THEY ACCUMULATE DURING THEIR LIFETIME DETERMINES WHETHER THEY ARE REBORN INTO A LOWER OR A HIGHER REALM.

Above 'The Burning Cauldron', a section from the 12th-century Japanese Hell Scrolls, *which depict 7 of the 16 lesser hells described in the* Sutra of the World Arising.

Buddhists see the universe as consisting of three worlds or spheres, which are inhabited by beings living out their cycles of birth–death–rebirth. The lowest is the Sphere of the Senses and Desires; above it is the Sphere of Form – the world of subtle matter; and the highest is called the Sphere of Formlessness – the realm of incorporeal beings. The spheres are subdivided into 31 levels, or realms, each inhabited by a different category of being. The lowest realm is Hell, while at the top is a heaven of Neither Perception nor Non-Perception. Here consciousness is transcended and only the mind exists.

SPHERES OF REBIRTH

It is possible to be reborn into any realm, or sphere, of the Buddhist universe, since samsara, or the cycle of rebirth, takes place inside and between the three spheres. To be born into the Sphere of Formlessness is to be close to liberation, but it is also possible for inhabitants of the lower spheres to become enlightened. Those who attain enlightenment no longer inhabit the spheres of existence.

To be reborn as a human, high up in the Sphere of the Senses and Desires, is a beneficial destiny for any being, because humans have ample opportunity to make spiritual progress toward achieving enlightenment and thus ending the cycle of samsara. However, those who have accumulated 'good' karma may be reborn at a higher level. To be reborn into one of the many levels inhabited by the gods is a challenge: existence there is blissful, yet gods must still strive to attain enlightenment and escape samsara. If they do not, they may be reborn into a lower sphere.

Below the human realm are the realms of 'bad destiny', where beings who have accumulated

Left The six segments of the Wheel of Life represent the six realms of rebirth in the Buddhist universe. Clockwise: 1. Gods, 2. Titans, 3. Animals, 4. Hell, 5. Ghosts, 6. Humans.

Above This Thai temple painting shows the Buddha visiting his mother in one of the lower of the 26 heavens of the Buddhist universe, and afterward descending to Earth.

'bad' karma may be reborn. The lowest realm consists of various hells, where evil deeds are punished by torments such as fire and freezing. In the Buddhist universe, once evil deeds have been expiated, release follows, and beings are reborn into a higher realm.

To be reborn into the animal kingdom is undesirable, since animals, whose understanding is limited and whose lives may be naturally short, or shortened by predators, have little opportunity to achieve enlightenment. Ghosts – former humans driven by insatiable cravings – inhabit the third realm and, some scriptures claim, there is a fourth realm inhabited by warlike Titans, who are enslaved by attachment to violence and power.

LEVELS OF MEDITATION

Meditation is the central practice in almost every school of Buddhism because it provides a superhighway to enlightenment. Novices begin with exercises in concentration and mind control, but once they have achieved deep states of trance, called dhyanas, they enter the Sphere of Form. As they master advanced meditation techniques, they may pass from these lower levels and enter the Sphere of Formlessness, where they may attain the meditation levels of Infinite Space, Infinite Consciousness, or even higher.

The Pali texts and later scriptures record that the Buddha managed to reach the seventh and eighth levels – the Realm of Nothingness, where body and mind separate, and of Neither Perception nor Non-Perception – which are on the same plane as the highest levels of the Buddhist universe. From there, he passed into nirvana.

THE WHEEL OF LIFE

The Wheel of Life (Bhavacakra, literally 'Wheel of Becoming') represents samsara. At its hub are a pig, a snake and a cock. These are the 'Three Poisons' that hinder spiritual development. The pig symbolizes greed, the snake hatred and the cock delusion. Delusions are negative traits, such as ill will, stubbornness, worry and laziness. The three animals pursue each other, keeping the wheel in motion. Delusions are obstacles to enlightenment, and individuals must overcome their negative traits or remain in samsara.

Rebirths are shown in the circle around the hub of the wheel: the right, black half depicts figures falling into the 'bad destinies', from which rebirth is almost inevitable, and the left half shows the ascent into levels of existence that offer hope of liberation.

Yama, Lord of Death, whose three eyes symbolize impermanence, harm and non-self, grasps the wheel. His five skulls represent freedom from old age, sickness, death, decay and rebirth.

Below A detail from a Wheel of Life illustration shows the central disc and the black-and-white circle around it.

REBECOMING

CENTRAL TO THE DHARMA IS THE CONCEPT OF SAMSARA, THE CYCLE OF BIRTH, AGEING, DEATH AND REBIRTH – THE IDEA THAT, JUST AS THE FLAME OF A DYING CANDLE SETS A NEW CANDLE BURNING, AT THE DEATH OF A LIVING BEING A NEW ONE COMES INTO EXISTENCE.

"Whatever things have an origin must come to cessation", taught the Buddha. At the end of life, the body dies, and the components that make up the personality dissolve. He did not teach that the personality, or even the soul, lives on after death to be reborn in a new body. His words are often explained by the analogy of a candle: just as a dying flame can light a new candle, so the dissolution of one personality

Below Tibetan monks accompany a deceased lama (a Tibetan teacher of the Dharma) to the cremation oven. Attending cremations, and even autopsies, keeps Buddhist monks mindful of the teaching of anitya, *or impermanence.*

gives rise to another. "There is rebirth of character", explained the Buddha to a Brahmin who asked if his soul would be reborn, "but no transmigration of a self. The thought-forms reappear, but there is no ego-entity transferred. The stanza uttered by a teacher is reborn in the scholar who repeats the words."

IMPERMANENCE

Buddhism celebrates the happiness that youth, success, friendship, love and parenthood can bring, but happiness is not the Buddhist goal. The Buddha-Dharma instils the message of *anitya*, or impermanence: youth, excitement, joy, contentment pass away; sorrow and sickness dog the lives of many,

Above The cycle of samsara (which translates from Sanskrit as 'the wandering') is started again at birth. Being born into the human realm is fortunate, and offers the opportunity of eventual enlightenment.

and bereavement and death are inevitable. All these experiences are *duhkha* – forms of suffering that range from dissatisfaction to misery, pain and grief. If we wish to understand the reality of our existence, we must recognize, as

36

Above The Bodhisattva Maitreya is an enlightened being, but out of compassion for humankind he waits in his heaven to be reborn on Earth as the future Buddha.

Above Hells form the lowest level of existence in the Buddhist universe. This Khmer relief from Angkor Wat shows servants of Yama, Deva of Death, stringing up and beating those in debt to evil.

did the young Siddhartha Gautama when he encountered old age, sickness and death, that suffering is inescapable. Further, if living and dying bring suffering, then repeated living and dying must bring the greatest suffering.

KARMA

Buddhist thought does not see suffering as punishment for having offended a god or gods. The Dharma teaches that people's unhappiness and suffering are the effect of their own harmful actions. The moral choices people make consciously and intentionally impact on their futures, and in this way individuals shape their own destinies. Bad actions, such as violence, greed, hatred and selfishness, harm others and also those who commit them. The resulting karma accumulates through a lifetime and must be expiated by suffering. No buddha can forgive it, and it does not expire when the body dies. It lives on after death, eventually to be reborn.

HEAVENS AND HELLS

The Buddha's last words were "Decay is inherent in all component things". Even death and rebirth are impermanent. After death, unenlightened living beings enter into one of five or six forms of rebirth, depending on their karma. They can be reborn in a hell – a place not of damnation but of purification, where evil deeds committed during earthly existence are punished by torment. When the evil is expiated, the being is released, to be reborn into a higher realm. Beings can be reborn as any kind of animal life, a ghost, a human or a god.

Reborn beings inhabit any of 31 realms, or states of existence, in the Buddhist universe. The upper realms are heavens, the mansions of the gods. Animals, humans, even the gods in their multi-level heavens, are all subject to the law of the Dharma and must attain enlightenment to end the cycle of death and rebirth that results from karmic cause and effect.

THE IDEA OF REINCARNATION

Buddhists speak of 'rebirth', 'rebecoming' or 're-death' rather than 'reincarnation', which has a narrower meaning: the rebirth of the soul in another body. In Hindu doctrine, for example, the immortal soul, or *atman*, is repeatedly reborn in the body of a living being. "Worn-out garments are shed by the body. Worn-out bodies are shed by the dweller within the body. New bodies are donned by the dweller, like garments", declares the *Bhagavadgita*, an important Hindu text. Achieving moksha, or enlightenment, frees the soul from reincarnation. The Buddha-Dharma shares the idea of rebirth with the Hindus, Jains and Sikhs, but rejects the idea of an immortal soul that lives on, unchanging, after death, as well as the belief that humans are reborn only as humans. They may be reborn as animals, or as ghosts – disembodied former humans whose worldly desires made them slaves to attachment.

Above Just as new star clusters, such as the Pleiades, form from the dust of dying stars, so everything in the Buddhist universe passes through a cycle of birth, death and rebirth.

CAUSE AND EFFECT

TO WIN FREEDOM FROM THE CONSEQUENCES OF PAST KARMA, A PERSON MUST BREAK, ONE BY ONE, EVERY LINK IN THE CHAIN OF KARMIC CAUSE AND EFFECT. THIS IS ACHIEVED BY MEANS OF MORAL DECISIONS, MERITORIOUS LIVING, DAILY PRACTICE AND MEDITATION.

Central to Buddhist thinking is the idea of karma, meaning 'deeds'. All actions have future consequences in terms of personal merit (*punya*, or 'good' karma) or demerit (*papa*, or 'bad' karma). A kindness to another person accumulates merit by building *punya*, while a selfish, unkind act will earn demerit through *papa*. However, Buddhists believe that for actions to have karmic consequences, they must be carried out consciously and intentionally.

The balance of karma at death determines in which of the six realms of the Buddhist universe (shown on the preceding pages) an individual will be reborn. Karma is also thought to determine one's physical appearance, health, mental abilities and character. Bad deeds, such as lying or theft, shape one's character and destiny after death. Thus, the Buddha taught, we are responsible for our own salvation.

Below An illustration from the Sutra of Cause and Effect, *detailing the incarnations of the Buddha. Here, men report to Siddhartha's father that he is following his new life of austerity.*

THE 12 STEPS TO REBIRTH

The Buddha analysed how karmic cause and effect works in his doctrine of *pratitya-samutpada*, a concept which is variously translated as 'dependent arising', or 'co-dependent origination', or 'origination-in-dependence'. This idea means that an event takes place only because other events exist in a chain of cause and effect that extends both into the past and the future. Thus, if X happens, Y will follow; if X does not happen, then Y will not follow.

The chain has 12 links or steps, each of which comes into existence because of the preceding one. The 12 segments in the outer circle of the Wheel of Life illustrate in sequence the links in this chain of cause and effect:

1 Cause and effect start from ignorance, the first link in the chain. Ignorance is represented by a blind man, because men are blinded by their own ignorance.

2 A potter at his wheel follows the blind man as the second link in the chain. The potter represents the individual shaping his life in ignorance by his actions.

Above The Wheel of Life depicts the sequence of 12 events in the chain of cause and effect. The sequence leads to samsara – the cycle of birth–death– rebirth. Samsara will end only if the chain is broken.

3 A monkey represents the imprints of actions taken in ignorance on the consciousness, parts of which survive death and carry them into a future life.

4 Travellers in a boat symbolize the consciousness ('name') that enters the embryo in the womb of the individual's future mother. The boat represents the body ('form') that the embryo will become.

5 Empty houses in link 5 represent the six soon-to-develop senses of the embryo.

6 A couple holding each other symbolizes contact. The six senses of the growing infant develop to the stage where communication becomes possible.

7 A man shot in the eye is the image on the seventh segment of the Wheel of Life. It symbolizes the ability of the embryo's maturing senses to transmit pain and pleasure. Through these feelings, individuals experience karma directly, by responding to the effects of their past actions, both good and bad.

8 An individual eating an apple symbolizes the feelings of desire caused by attachment.

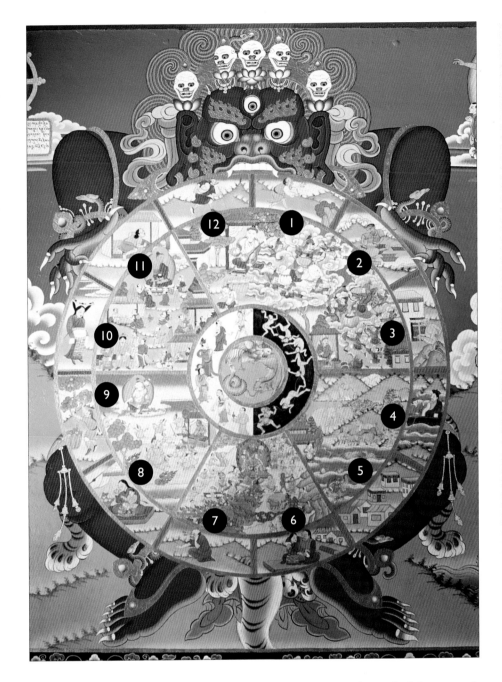

DELUSIONS

The negative traits that haunt behaviour and destroy peace of mind are called *kleshas* (literally 'passions'), translated as afflictive or conflicting emotions, or delusions. The *kleshas* are the thoughtless reactions – laziness, for example, or restlessness, anxiety, scepticism, indecisiveness, pride or conceit, stubbornness, impatience, irritation and ill will – that can seem to drive behaviour. In certain situations, they take over, obscuring our vision of ourselves and of reality, so that we are forced to deal with the world through them. They include the 'Three Poisons' – ignorance, hatred and delusion – that keep the Wheel of Life spinning. *Kleshas* drive us to actions that cause suffering to others and ourselves, and are a manifestation of attachment: I want/I don't want.

The way to banish *kleshas* is twofold. First, they must be dealt with through meditation, increasing one's awareness of each delusion by observing it. Second, negative traits must be replaced with positive ones. The way to achieve this is to cultivate the Buddhist virtues, which include unselfishness, kindness, benevolence and compassion – an understanding of human suffering.

Above The outer circle of the Wheel of Life depicts the 12 links in the chain of causation that leads to samsara. Starting in the top right-hand segment (at one o'clock), the numbered links follow each other in sequence clockwise around the mandala.

9 A man snatching fruit out of a tree represents grasping – the response to attachment. This ninth link symbolizes the delusion of strong attachment to the self.

10 The pregnant woman is a symbol of new life. Grasping and attachment strengthen at death and ripen in the mind into seeds of the karma, which are carried into the next existence.

11 A woman in childbirth symbolizes the ripening of the seeds of karma as an individual's elements are reborn.

12 The process of life, growth, development, decay and re-death begins even at conception. In this final link on the Wheel of Life, the individual is represented by a person carrying a heavy bundle, which is symbolic of the burden of karma that the individual created during past lives.

During the process of his enlightenment, which, the scriptures say, took one night, the Buddha unlocked each link in this chain of cause and effect, thus ending samsara. This was an achievement that, it is believed, would normally take three successive lifetimes.

THE FOUR NOBLE TRUTHS

IN HIS FIRST SERMON AFTER ENLIGHTENMENT, THE BUDDHA TAUGHT HIS DISCIPLES THE FOUR NOBLE TRUTHS. THESE TRUTHS ARE THE FOUNDATION OF HIS PHILOSOPHY, THE KERNEL OF DOCTRINE THAT EVERY NEWCOMER TO BUDDHISM MUST KNOW AND ACCEPT.

1 TO LIVE IS TO SUFFER

The reality of *duhkha* is the first truth. *Duhkha* (Pali: *dukkha*) is commonly translated as 'suffering', but there are many kinds of suffering, ranging from unease to sorrow. *Duhkha* may be physical pain, illness, bereavement, despair, or psychological pain. It is also the disruption to happiness caused all through life by *anitya*, or impermanence, such as the ending of love. "Birth is suffering", preached the Buddha in the Deer Park at Isipatana, "illness is suffering, ageing is suffering, death is suffering.

Below The Buddha chose to remain on Earth after enlightenment to teach the Four Noble Truths to humanity. This 8th-century Japanese sutra (scripture) shows the incarnation of the Buddha burning after his bodily death.

To be united with the unpleasant is suffering, separation from the pleasant is suffering. Desire that remains unsatisfied is suffering."

2 ATTACHMENT IS THE CAUSE OF SUFFERING

All suffering is caused by craving and greed. The Sanskrit word for suffering is *trishna* (Pali: *tanha*). Its literal meaning is 'thirst', but it is commonly translated as 'desire' or 'attachment'. There is attachment to sensual pleasures, craving for material possessions, and greed for personal gain in terms of wealth, influence, power, or fame. Some people crave eternal youth and immortality; others desire an end to life.

All these cravings distort thinking and perception, shielding the mind from reality, and may result in lying, theft, degradation,

Above The Scream by Edvard Munch expresses the tension of existential suffering, the duhkha *that builds up through life as a result of its inevitable failures, frustrations and disappointments.*

oppression of others, hatred and even murder. These actions cause others to suffer, but experiencing craving is itself suffering. Unfulfilled cravings are painful, but the satisfaction or exhilaration of fulfilled cravings is usually short-lived and is replaced by a sense of loss, a form of suffering that causes renewed desire. In his

SANSKRIT TERMS

In Buddhism, the three marks of existence are:

anatman non-self, no soul – the doctrine that there is no immortal spirit at the core of any living being.

anitya impermanence, the view that nothing lasts and that all phenomena will eventually pass away.

duhkha suffering of every type, ranging from unease and lack of satisfaction with life to physical and mental pain.

Above Following the Middle Way brings detachment from craving and opens the mind to reality and an understanding of oneself and the world.

ATTACHMENT

Craving chocolate, cigarettes, alcohol or tranquillizers; the urge to consume; clinging to people; wanting to make more money than anyone else, or to have the coolest car or the latest fashions – these things ultimately cause suffering. The Middle Way prevails in all the Buddha's teachings, so normal wanting and needing are not the root cause of suffering. Desiring to make new friends, buy a winter coat, or spend time with family and friends are not examples of craving. Never wanting to be alone, shopping till you drop, pursuing power for the sake of it and being irrationally jealous are what the Buddha called "Burning with the fire of desire...the fire of delusion". Behaviour driven by burning desire is suffering because it stifles empathy and compassion, warps the mind and can never really be satisfied. In the 21st-century world, *trishna*, magnified by advertising and marketing campaigns, has a magnetic hold on people.

teachings, the Buddha counselled against gratifying the senses and giving free reign to the passions.

3 THERE CAN BE AN END TO SUFFERING

In the Buddha's teaching, there is a message of hope: that suffering can be brought to an end. If attachment, selfish desires and cravings are ultimately the cause of all suffering, then it follows that eradicating them will cause suffering to cease. However, this means going back to their roots and eradicating ignorance – of oneself, of how things are, of the Four Noble Truths. Ignorance is symbolized by the pig that chases the cock (symbol of attachment) and the snake (symbol of aversion) at the centre of the Wheel of Life, so keeping it turning.

The Buddha taught that the disciple who sees things as they are becomes dispassionate toward them. "Being dispassionate, this disciple becomes detached and, through detachment, is liberated."

Attaining nirvana – extinguishing the flame of repeated births and deaths – is the end of all suffering.

4 A PATH LEADS TO THE CESSATION OF SUFFERING

The way to end suffering is, as Siddhartha Gautama learned during his years as a *shramana*, the Middle Way between heedless self-indulgence and extreme self-denial. It is the way along the Noble Eightfold Path that leads the seeker to nirvana. These eight steps to enlightenment were taught by the Buddha in his First Sermon in the Deer Park at Isipatana.

THE NOBLE EIGHTFOLD PATH

TO FOLLOW THE NOBLE EIGHTFOLD PATH IS HARD, BUT AS THE MIDDLE WAY, IT REQUIRES RENUNCIATION AND SELF-DISCIPLINE, NOT SELF-TORTURE. THE WAY OFFERS CALM AND INNER PEACE, INSIGHT AND WISDOM, AND LEADS EVENTUALLY TO NIRVANA.

As he set the Wheel of the Dharma in motion, the Buddha turned to his followers: "And what, monks, is this middle course fully awakened to by the Truthfinder", he asked them, "making for vision, making for knowledge, which conduces to calming, to superknowledge, to awakening, to nirvana? It is the… eightfold way itself."

Part of the initiation into Buddhism is a declaration of faith in the Four Noble Truths and the Noble Eightfold Path, which form the essence of Buddhist doctrine.

Below The Dharmachakra *is the Wheel of the Law. It has eight spokes, each representing a step on the Noble Eightfold Path to enlightenment.*

The first two steps along the Eightfold Path develop wisdom; steps three to five teach moral living; and six to eight train the mind for meditation.

1 RIGHT VIEW
Recognizing the truth of the Buddha's teachings and accepting them is the first stage on the path to enlightenment. That means understanding and accepting the Four Noble Truths, of which the last is the Noble Eightfold Path. What is asked is not blind faith – the Buddha advised the Sangha to question everything – but an acceptance that the Dharma is worth personal commitment. Each Truth is expressed concisely, yet understanding all four involves

Above Meditation is central to Buddhist practice. It helps to deepen understanding of the Four Noble Truths and the Noble Eightfold Path.

mental effort. Buddhist monks spend a lifetime deepening their understanding of the Four Truths and the Eightfold Path through discourse, reading and meditation. The right view is the right understanding or knowledge. In time, the practitioner begins to see the world as it truly is, undistorted by illusion.

2 RIGHT RESOLVE
The essence of Buddhist doctrine is that people can and must change, for the right change can end samsara. Right resolve is a commitment to a process of change, which begins with developing right attitudes, such as an intention to free oneself from attachment to worldly pleasures, to eradicate selfishness and to replace them with sensitivity, empathy and compassion.

3 RIGHT SPEECH
This step means telling the truth. Part of learning to see things as they really are is to recognize the

truth as it is, undistorted by ego, and to cease embroidering it or presenting it in a way that furthers one's interests.

Right speech is thoughtful. It means weighing up one's words so they are not frivolous, insensitive, angry or sarcastic. Speaking ill of others harms them, so silence is better than gossip. The scriptures recount the divisive talk of Devadatta, the Buddha's cousin, who, from jealousy and frustrated ambition, tried to turn members of the Sangha against the Buddha.

4 RIGHT ACTION

Buddhists strive to do nothing that could harm other living beings. Such wrong actions range from killing, stealing ("do not take what is not given") and committing sexual acts that could have harmful consequences, to smaller acts of injury, dishonesty and the abuse of sensual pleasures. The injunction not to kill living beings is interpreted by many Buddhists as a ban on eating meat.

Right action is pivotal in training the mind in right thinking, in the sense that right view, right effort and right mindfulness are bound up with it. "One tries to abandon wrong action and enter into right action: This is one's right effort. One is mindful to abandon wrong action and to enter and remain in right action: This is one's right mindfulness", read the scriptures.

5 RIGHT LIVELIHOOD

This, the third of the steps that teach moral living, rules out work that harms others or hampers one's spiritual progress. A Buddhist's occupation should not infringe right speech and right action.

Some ancient texts single out the arms trade, slavery, dealing in flesh – for example, the slaughter of animals – and trade in

Above Debating Buddhist scriptures is a way to develop right speech. It forms an important part of the daily training of Tibetan Buddhist monks.

intoxicating drink and poisons, such as illegal drugs. Those trades still flourish and Buddhists today are forbidden from being butchers, hunters or executioners. Life is now more complicated, however, so dealers in stocks and shares issued by companies involved in unethical trades, retailers selling goods produced by unethical labour policies, and anyone engaged in business activities that harm the environment and so threaten the survival of living beings, may be seen as examples of wrongful ways of making a living.

6 RIGHT EFFORT

Effort has to be applied to banish harmful states of mind, such as jealousy, covetousness, greed and melancholy. This means learning to control one's negative thoughts and encouraging and instilling positive thinking, especially qualities such as kindness and empathy.

Right effort supports right action and requires that the mind be prepared for meditation, for right effort requires mental energy. Daily practice purifies the thoughts and so releases mental energy for sustained concentration.

7 RIGHT MINDFULNESS

Mindfulness is presence of mind, attentiveness, being aware of what is going on in the present. This second stage of preparation for meditation involves the cultivation of constant self-awareness – of the body, the mind and thought processes, and the feelings. Practising right mindfulness, one becomes aware of the transient nature of thoughts, bodily sensations, feelings, wants and cravings – the impermanence of all things. Constant vigilance of thought, speech and action strengthens the mind, making it easier to cultivate mindfulness. The aim is to discipline the mind to achieve steady concentration.

8 RIGHT CONCENTRATION

Meditation is the eighth step on the path. Achieving right concentration means reaching the stage of being able to calm the mind and concentrate on one object, subject or theme. This involves practising meditation techniques.

THE FIVE PRECEPTS

ALL BUDDHISTS OBSERVE THE FIVE PRECEPTS. THESE ARE NOT LAWS
LAID DOWN BY ANY GOD, NOR A VOW TO ANY SUPERNATURAL BEING,
BUT A PROMISE TO ONESELF TO OBSERVE EACH RULE, THE AIM
BEING TO DIMINISH ATTACHMENT TO HARMFUL PRACTICES.

An important part of the
Noble Eightfold Path,
implicit in right action, right
speech and right livelihood, is the
need to live a moral, virtuous life.
Dishonesty and immorality hurt
others and have a harmful effect
on those who commit them in
that they leave a negative imprint
on the consciousness. This inhibits
the attainment of wisdom and
insight and hence the ability to
achieve enlightenment.

*Below Monks dress statues at
Borobudur in saffron robes. The first
Buddhist monks adopted saffron robes
because they were worn by the poor.*

Committing acts that transgress
the law of Dharma, which
governs the universe, results in
the continuation of the cycle of
death and rebirth, and hence suffering, through the accumulation
of 'bad' karma.

RULES FOR LIVING

The Buddha established a number
of basic rules of conduct for his
followers. The most important of
these have been preserved as the
Pancasila, the Five Precepts that all
lay followers must accept on
becoming Buddhists. By making a
solemn commitment to observe
the Five Precepts and follow the

*Above A respect for living creatures is
enshrined in the First Precept. Buddhists
are prohibited from professions that
involve the intentional killing of animals.*

Eightfold Path, one reduces the
danger of committing acts that
will increase negative karma.

1 TO REFRAIN FROM INJURING LIVING BEINGS

"Whosoever strives only for his
own happiness, and in so doing
hurts or kills living creatures

which also seek for happiness, he shall find no happiness after death", states the *Dharmapada*, a text of the Pali canon.

This first precept requires that Buddhists treat other creatures with compassion and kindness informed by an understanding of the relationship between all living things. The extension of this injunction to all forms of life, including vermin and harmful creatures, can pose ethical conundrums for Buddhists.

2 TO REFRAIN FROM STEALING

Literally "to refrain from taking what is not given", this involves all forms of stealing, including stealing time from one's employer and engaging in dubious business practices, to coveting someone else's boyfriend or wife. Tied in with this precept is the idea that those who acquire wealth should not cling to it but use it for the benefit of humanity.

3 TO REFRAIN FROM SEXUAL IMMORALITY

All Buddhists are urged not to cause harm to others or themselves through enslavement to sexual indulgence. The attraction of the body is transient and training oneself to manage the powerful sexual urge – to deflect it in the direction of creativity, perhaps – is to make an important advance in banishing the second of the 'Three Poisons' that keep the cycle of samsara in motion.

4 TO REFRAIN FROM LYING

To follow the way of the Truth necessarily demands the truth in thought, word and deed. The Fourth Precept requires that one brings tendencies to exaggeration and inaccuracy under control, together with the habit of speaking ill of other people.

5 TO REFRAIN FROM INTOXICANTS

'Intoxicants' include alcohol and recreational drugs, and indeed anything that clouds the mind and prevents one from living in the present and seeing things as they really are, however painful that may be. Most schools and teachers take the Fifth Precept very seriously, but some commentators consider it to be less important than the other four because some texts omit it.

Above A detail of a wheel of life, showing the 'Three Poisons' in the middle keeping the wheel turning. The foot of Yama, the personification of Death, can be seen protruding at the bottom of the wheel.

By making a solemn commitment to observe the Five Precepts and follow the Noble Eightfold Path, one reduces the danger of committing acts that will increase negative karma.

MERIT

Rebirth into a higher realm of the Buddhist universe and the duration of an individual's stay there before rebirth depend on the balance of 'good' and 'bad' karma accumulated during life. Right actions, such as charity, moral conduct and meditation, hearing Dharma talks, attending religious events and making pilgrimages to holy sights, all earn *punya*, or merit, which increases one's balance of 'good' karma. Anything that helps overcome the 'Three Poisons' (ignorance, delusion and hatred), including observing the Five Precepts, acquires merit. Actions taken with good intentions sometimes cause harm, but if the intention was genuine, the consequences of the action do not produce 'bad' karma. However, actions carried out with the intention of earning karma points, rather than a genuine desire to help the afflicted and attain enlightenment, are unlikely to earn 'good' karma.

Right Monks go out each morning to collect food. This is not begging, but rather allowing lay people the opportunity to earn karmic merit by giving.

THE TRIPLE REFUGE

RECITING THREE SIMPLE STATEMENTS CALLED THE 'TRIPLE REFUGE' CONFIRMS A PERSON'S CONVERSION TO BUDDHISM, AND IT IS ALSO A DECLARATION OF CONTINUING COMMITMENT: BUDDHISTS RECITE THE TRIPLE REFUGE ON HOLY DAYS AND BEFORE DAILY MEDITATION.

Each Buddhist tradition has its own ceremonies for receiving new members. Some are complex. In Tibetan Buddhism, for example, newcomers must undergo specific initiation to be able to take part in certain introductory practices. But all traditions will at some stage require new members to make these statements:

I take refuge in the Buddha.

~

I take refuge in the Dharma.

~

I take refuge in the Sangha.

Reciting these declarations, called the Triple Refuge, is the minimum required to become a Buddhist. They may simply be spoken three times by an individual, who should also read and understand the Four Noble Truths, follow the Noble Eightfold Path and observe the Five Precepts (not to harm living creatures, not to steal, to refrain from sexual immorality, not to lie and not to take intoxicants). But it is better to recite or chant the Triple Refuge in the presence of a member of the Sangha, or as part of a group. Becoming a Buddhist – a renunciant – is a solemn commitment, and it is appropriate to celebrate it with some ceremony.

TAKING REFUGE

After his enlightenment, the scriptures recount how the Buddha accepted food offered to him by two foreign merchants.

Above Mañjushri is the Bodhisattva of Wisdom. His right hand wields a flaming sword, symbolizing wisdom cutting through ignorance and wrong views. In his left hand, he holds a scripture, symbolic of enlightenment.

In return, the Buddha granted them refuge in himself and his teachings. Soon afterward, the five ascetics to whom he preached his First Sermon became the nucleus of the first Buddhist community. This marked the formation of the first Sangha, and some weeks later, the father of Yashas, a young bhikkhu (monk), became the first lay follower to take the Triple Refuge.

To 'take refuge' means to renounce one's former dependence on worldly possessions and achievements for happiness – dependence on social position, for example, earning power, career, or even friends and family – and to trust one's spiritual welfare and future progress and happiness to the 'Three Treasures' (another term for the Triple Refuge, which is also called the Triple Gem).

Left The triratna is the symbol of the Triple Refuge, also called the Three Treasures, the Three Jewels, and the Triple Gem. This Gandharan frieze shows the triratna beneath the Dharma Wheel on the Buddha's footprints.

THREE PRECIOUS THINGS

The Buddha, the Dharma and the Sangha are so precious that they are often represented in Buddhist art as jewels. Each one is invested with many layers of meaning.

1 THE BUDDHA

Having experienced life's comforts and sensual excitements, yet renounced them in order to seek the untrodden path to *bodhi*, the Buddha is a spiritual ideal to follow. To 'take refuge in the Buddha' is to find peace of mind in his example and to learn from his understanding of the nature of reality at times when life ceases to satisfy or becomes painful.

2 THE DHARMA

The ancient law of the universe and morality was the Truth the Buddha rediscovered during his enlightenment. His awakening enabled him to see things as they really are. To 'take refuge in the Dharma' is to accept the Buddha's teachings as a guide for how to live. It offers counsel to those who seek advice, and knowledge of the

Right The Triple Refuge is depicted as three 'baskets', symbolizing stores of knowledge, in this thangka *in the Pemayangtse monastery, India.*

nature of reality for those in a quest for guidance on the path to nirvana.

3 THE SANGHA

It is difficult to make steady spiritual progress alone. Concentration is difficult to achieve and all individuals have shortcomings that impede their advancement. The experienced leaders of the Sangha help individuals find the path to enlightenment. To take refuge in the Sangha is to accept support, criticism, help and advice from a community of people who share the same goal.

The true qualities of Buddha, Dharma and Sangha are called 'the Mirror of the Dharma', and reflecting on them is a practice aimed at attaining a 'mind like a mirror'. This helps the meditator develop those qualities and so attain the first stage of enlightenment, or become a 'stream-enterer'.

LAY FOLLOWERS

The Buddhist Sangha consists of bhikkhus and bhikkhunis (monks and nuns), who are forbidden to work for money, and lay people who commit themselves to the Triple Refuge. Lay followers do not aspire to attain nirvana through monastic discipline and meditation, but earn merit through *dana*, or giving. They support the monastic community materially, not only by putting food into the bowls of bhikkhus and bhikkhunis each morning but also by donating tea, cotton cloth for robes, flowers, incense and other items, and money for the monks to build and maintain monasteries and carry out charitable works. (In Cambodia, Thailand and other Buddhist countries, religious communities care for people with AIDS and their orphaned children, for example.) The laity also observe the Five Precepts and make pilgrimages to holy sites, an action that earns merit. Monks and nuns practise *dana* by giving talks on the Dharma to lay members on the twice-monthly holy days.

Right In some countries Buddhist parents send their boys from the age of seven to spend the rainy season at a temple. They take part in ceremonies and receive religious education and moral and spiritual training.

THE GOURMET BUDDHIST

AS AN ASCETIC SEARCHING FOR THE PATH TO ENLIGHTENMENT, SIDDHARTHA GAUTAMA LEARNED THAT EXTREME SELF-DENIAL COULD NOT HELP HIM REACH HIS GOAL. IT WAS THE MIDDLE WAY BETWEEN ASCETICISM AND INDULGENCE THAT LED HIM TO NIRVANA.

Above Some scriptures of the Mahayana tradition advocate vegetarianism. Indeed, many Buddhists become vegetarians so that they do not develop a callous attitude toward other creatures and also to cultivate compassion and loving kindness.

The Buddha learned from experience that he needed a healthy body to achieve enlightenment. He therefore taught his followers not to starve themselves and, likewise, not to overindulge. The sixth of the ten moral precepts to which Buddhist monks and nuns still adhere is: eat one simple meal a day, before noon, and only liquids after midday.

VEGETARIANISM

The first of the Pancasila – the Five Precepts all Buddhists must observe – is to avoid killing or harming any living thing. This precept has always been the source of much controversy among Buddhists as to whether they should eat meat. Scriptures record that the Buddha ate meat and he did not make vegetarianism a rule for his disciples to follow. Indeed, the rule was that they should eat whatever they were offered by the public, whether or not they approved of it or liked it. The Middle Way also counselled that rather than starve, Buddhists should eat meat, but in the *Vanijja Sutta*, a Pali scripture, dealing in flesh is listed as one of the livelihoods proscribed by the Buddha in the Noble Eightfold Path.

Monastic rules state that monks and nuns of the Theravada tradition should eat meat placed in their begging bowls, as long as the animal was not killed for them. Buddhists of the Mahayana tradition argue that animals suffer in the production of meat, so that vegetarianism must be seen as the only compassionate solution.

Left "Let him neither kill, nor cause to be killed any living being...", states the Sutta Nipata, *part of the Pali canon. No compassionate person, it is felt, could condone killing simply for enjoyment, as in blood sports. This image of a hare hunt is from a French 15th-century manuscript.*

Left A statue of the Buddha during his period of meditation and fasting, from the Dungeshwari caves in Bodhgaya, India. Starving oneself is an ascetic practice that was frowned upon by the Buddha. Becoming too thin is as much an impediment to enlightenment as overeating.

loss of control, which can be dangerous. Dealing in intoxicants is one of the 'wrong livelihoods' specified by the Buddha, according to the *Vanijja Sutta*.

'Drugs' is usually deemed to mean nicotine as well as narcotics and the non-narcotics, such as marijuana and psychedelic drugs. Some commentators also include the caffeine in foods and drinks, such as chocolate, tea and coffee.

Several scriptures omit the Fifth Precept, while others emphasize the need to prevent the slothfulness drugs cause. No one needs alcohol to stay healthy, but sick people may need drugs to combat illness. The ideal is perfect mental, moral and physical control.

Below Monks and nuns traditionally eat food donated by lay Buddhists. They must eat what they are given, whether or not they like it. They eat no solid food after noon.

Buddhists today must consider these same arguments. Some might be equally concerned not to consume eggs or the milk of animals that have been reared inhumanely, fruit and vegetables produced by exploiting farmers in developing countries, or grain and pulses grown to the detriment of the environment.

Healthy food is a further consideration. Modern Buddhists need to weigh up the health effects of convenience foods high in sugar, fats, additives and stimulants.

INTOXICANTS

The Fifth Precept says, "I undertake to refrain from intoxicants, which lead to heedlessness." This is common sense, state the commentators, because the path to enlightenment requires clarity and presence of mind. Alcoholic drink and recreational drugs cloud the mind and, in excess, they cause

THE THREE CARDINAL VIRTUES

MANY VIRTUOUS CHARACTER TRAITS AND THEIR OPPOSITES, VICES, ARE MENTIONED IN THE BUDDHIST TEXTS. TO OVERCOME THE THREE POISONS – IGNORANCE, HATRED AND DELUSION – IT IS NECESSARY TO CULTIVATE THEIR OPPOSITES, THE THREE CARDINAL VIRTUES.

Above A stone statue of Guanyin, the Buddhist goddess of compassion and mercy, from the Northern Wei dynasty, China, 552CE.

Virtue is the first step on the path to nirvana. As well as abstaining from evil and immoral deeds, Buddhists must train themselves to banish thoughts that are cruel, malevolent or unkind, dishonest or covetous, lustful or immoral. These bad habits of thought can obscure the perception of reality and in turn engender 'bad' karma. Eliminating negative character traits involves training the mind to replace them with more positive habits of thought and behaviour, such as giving and generosity. The most important Buddhist virtues are divided into three groups, which are known as the Three Cardinal Virtues. Buddhists believe that all other virtues emanate from these three.

1 NON-ATTACHMENT
This is the virtue of unselfishness. Buddhists strive to replace the desire to make one's own physical and psychological needs a priority with an impulse to think of others first. Part of this involves not looking to others to provide recognition of one's good intentions, actions or achievements.

2 BENEVOLENCE OR LOVING KINDNESS
This is goodwill toward all living beings. Early in meditation practice, Buddhists are asked to contemplate the consequences of the opposite of this virtue: anger, ill will and hatred. They then contrast those with the fruits of

Left In this Tibetan thangka, seven Medicine Buddhas represent the Buddha's power to heal suffering, using compassion and loving kindness.

COMPASSION

Karuna, or compassion, is the 'Law of Laws, eternal harmony'. Compassion is identification with and empathy toward life's many forms. All Buddhist traditions reject the notion that it is right for people to strive only for their own interests. This produces suffering. To embrace the concerns of other people and other forms of life is to work for the benefit of all life.

The Buddha delayed his passing into the bliss of nirvana out of compassion for humans who were struggling in ignorance, unaware of nirvana. The Mahayana tradition considered it wrong for monks to work for their own salvation and ignore the suffering of others, and elevated to the highest ideal the principle of service to the wellbeing of the world. An important aspect of seeing things as they are is recognizing and accepting one's own mortality and empathizing with the mortality of others.

Right Tara, an emanation of Avalokiteshvara, the Bodhisattva of Compassion, is depicted in this Sri Lankan temple painting. The 3 eyes in her head and those on the palms of her 12 hands enable her to see all human pain.

goodwill and its associated virtues: patience and forbearance. The next step is to shut out negative attitudes, from antipathy to ill will and anger, and replace them with benevolence, first to oneself, then outward to one's family, friends and colleagues, then to rivals and enemies, and finally to humankind and all life.

3 UNDERSTANDING

This is an awareness and comprehension of human suffering, as set out in the Four Noble Truths. The Buddha's recognition that all living beings suffer as a result of samsara is evidence of his extraordinary understanding. The second step on the Noble Eightfold Path, right resolve, promotes understanding of human nature and how it develops and changes, and of human good. The purpose of meditating on understanding is to bring oneself to desire the welfare and happiness of all beings.

FOUR HEAVENLY ABODES

The qualities of compassion, kindness, joy and equanimity, or peace of mind, are highly valued in Buddhism and carefully cultivated. These virtues are called the 'Heavenly Abodes' or the 'Four Immeasurables' (Pali: *Brahmavihara*).

Compassion is the partner of wisdom; it emanates from seeing reality and understanding life as a unity, changeable but indivisible, and oneself as subject to the same suffering as all other humans and other forms of life. Loving kindness is the natural response and it is cultivated by active concern for other people's problems and difficulties through everyday acts of generosity and by kindness.

The word 'charity' may bring to mind patronizing attitudes and assumptions of social and moral superiority. When compassion emanates from wisdom and is expressed through loving kindness, however, charity is offered with unconditional sympathy.

Bodhicitta is the name given in the Mahayana tradition to the compassionate motivation to attain enlightenment not for one's own salvation but solely to benefit others, whatever they might have done to cause them to remain trapped in samsara.

Below Phra Alongkot Tikhapanyo has founded a hospice in Thailand for HIV-positive children. Many Buddhist viharas help children orphaned by AIDS.

MEDITATION

AN ESSENTIAL PART OF BUDDHIST PRACTICE, MEDITATION CAN BRING ABOUT A TRANSFORMATION FROM NEGATIVE TO POSITIVE MENTAL STATES. IT PROMOTES THE PENETRATING INSIGHT AND UNDERSTANDING NEEDED TO ATTAIN ENLIGHTENMENT.

Meditation, or *bhavana*, which was a common practice among ascetics, was the tool the Buddha used to search for enlightenment, and it was during prolonged meditation that he achieved it. Meditation is therefore a central practice of all Buddhist schools and traditions.

To meditate is to bring about an altered state of consciousness in controlled ways that are conducive to liberation. Learning therefore involves becoming adept at a number of mind control techniques, starting with right mindfulness and right concentration – steps 6, 7 and 8 of

Below Monks spend much of their time alone in meditation, traditionally at dawn, midday and in the evening. This monk is at Sarnath, where the Buddha gave his First Sermon.

the Noble Eightfold Path. It is difficult for a beginner simply to concentrate – the mind wanders and extraneous thoughts grab the attention. For this reason, meditation is a serious discipline that requires daily practice. Until fairly recently in the Theravada tradition – an embodiment of the oldest Buddhist traditions – only monks practised meditation.

CALMING THE MIND

A commitment to regular practice brings rich rewards, nevertheless. To achieve right concentration, beginners might focus on the breathing, on repeating a mantra – a sacred word or saying – or they might observe in minute detail an object, such as a coloured disc or a flower, placed a few feet away. This was the meditative stage, *samadhi*, or trance meditation,

Above A buddha in walking meditation, radiating peace and serenity. His right hand, raised in the abhaya *mudra, symbolizes fearlessness; his left is extended in the gesture of giving, the* vadara *mudra.*

that the Buddha reached with his teachers. Trance meditation techniques achieve steady concentration on the object, and eventually absorption in it, so that the difference between 'I' and 'it' dissolves. This induces an exhilarated mental state, or dhyana. Trance meditation calms the mind to a state of deep inner stillness that can be blissful. These states of mind affect the personality generally, so that concentration, calmness and attention are heightened in everyday life.

INSIGHT

From calming meditation techniques, students may move on to *vipassana*, or insight meditation, following the steps of the Buddha, who left his teachers to work on meditation techniques that would

Above The dhyana mudra is a commonly used gesture of meditation. It symbolizes perfect balance of thought, peace and tranquillity, and concentration on the Dharma. It is also a comfortable position for the hands during seated meditation.

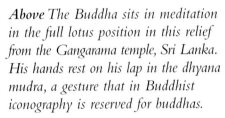

Above The Buddha sits in meditation in the full lotus position in this relief from the Gangarama temple, Sri Lanka. His hands rest on his lap in the dhyana mudra, a gesture that in Buddhist iconography is reserved for buddhas.

lead to enlightenment. Many Buddhist schools now teach only *vipassana*. This achieves knowledge derived from insight – not from flashes of insight but from a steady state of deep intuitive perception.

The meditator directs awareness first to the body, beginning with 'one-pointed' focus on the breathing, then going on to notice during meditation, but without making any response, every aspect of the anatomy and the sensations. This stage is called 'bare attention'. Later, the meditator will contemplate death and decay, attending cremations as well as meditating on corpses.

The second stage is to apply the same technique to the mind – its thoughts, moods, feelings. Person and personality are considered from the point of view of

the 'three marks of existence' – impermanence (*anitya*), suffering (*duhkha*) and non-self (*anatman*). Under this critical scrutiny thought patterns, such as desire, hatred and ignorance, reveal themselves and the thought processes that give rise to them become clear. To achieve this final stage, called 'clear comprehension',

involves mastering a complexity of techniques and can take many years.

Following the Noble Eightfold Path never stops being a prerequisite of meditation. Ceasing to strive for the right view or right resolve, or abandoning right action and right effort, affects the quality of meditation, no matter how advanced the meditator, and imposes an obstruction on the path to enlightenment for the disciple.

THE DHYANAS

Dhyanas are mental states or trance levels reached during meditation that correspond to the realms of the Buddhist universe, illustrated in the Wheel of Life.

The first level is a rapture that stems from success in calming and concentrating the mind to achieve 'one-pointed' meditation. The second-level meditator is adept at 'one-pointed' meditation, and elation is tempered by serenity and trust in the teaching. The third level is characterized by 'one-pointed' meditation and tranquil happiness. At the fourth level, happiness has subsided into equanimity, feeling is blanked out, and sharper mindfulness begins to break down the sense of self. Psychic powers appear, such as retrocognition – memory of past lives.

The Buddha transcended these levels, which are characterized by bodily awareness, and moved into the Sphere of Formlessness. From the fifth level, Infinite Space, and the sixth, Infinite Consciousness, he dissolved into Nothingness at the seventh, and passed from the eighth, the temporary end of consciousness and sensation, into nirvana.

ENLIGHTENMENT

BUDDHA MEANS 'AWAKENED', SO A BUDDHA IS A BEING WHO HAS ACHIEVED SPIRITUAL AWAKENING (*BODHI*). THIS STATE OF AWAKENING, USUALLY CALLED ENLIGHTENMENT – OR BY ITS SANSKRIT NAME, NIRVANA – IS THE GOAL OF BUDDHISTS OF ALL TRADITIONS.

Some people who have claimed to have entered nirvana have attempted to describe their experiences, and their efforts have always supported the truism that the experience of nirvana is ineffable: "I was the cosmos"; "I have forgotten the dread of birth and death". Nirvana is commonly defined as a state of perfect peace, bliss and heightened awareness. The Buddhist scriptures describe it as "the liberated mind that no longer clings", "the great, perfect mirror wisdom", or as the absence of anxiety, fear and doubt, a state

Below Parinirvana, from The Life of Buddha Sakyamuni. *Buddhists see parinirvana neither as death nor as an afterlife, but rather as the ultimate state of non-existence, from which there is no rebirth.*

of non-existence. The *Udana*, a book of the Pali canon, famously describes nirvana as the "Unborn, Unoriginated, Uncreated, Unformed."

'Nirvana' means 'extinction', in the sense of quenching thirst or blowing out a flame. What is extinguished is *trishna*, or desire. The implicit promise of the Third Noble Truth is that liberation will follow the complete cessation of desire: "the withdrawal from it, the renouncing of it, the rejection of it, liberation from it, non-attachment to it". What is also extinguished is samsara, the cycle of birth-death-rebirth. This occurs because the enlightened individual has gained full wisdom and succeeded in overcoming the *kleshas* – ignorance, hatred and delusion – replacing them with compassion and loving kindness, and is able to see existence as it is.

WISDOM

Prajna, meaning insight or wisdom, is the ability to understand the truth of reality, to see things as they really are. Its advanced attainment opens the door to nirvana. In some schools, notably Zen, prajna is equated with nirvana.

The attainment of wisdom begins with the Eightfold Path, since steps 1, right view (understanding the Four Noble Truths), and 2, right resolve (becoming detached from anger and hatred), are early steps in acquiring wisdom. Those following the Path must absorb the Dharma by listening to talks and sermons, studying sacred texts, engaging in discourse with colleagues and monks and, most important, banish the delusions that support the egotistical self. Wisdom is sharpened by meditation, particularly *vipassana* meditation, which interprets the truth in terms of the three marks of existence: *anitya*, (impermanence), *duhkha* (suffering), and *anatman*, non-self.

Above In Tantric rituals, a bell, symbol of wisdom, is held in the left hand. The bell is topped by the five spokes of a vajra *(thunderbolt), symbolizing the five forms of mystical wisdom.*

Above For two weeks after his enlightenment, the Buddha stood staring, unblinking, at the Bodhi tree, as depicted in this monumental rock carving in Polonnaruwa, Sri Lanka.

It was compassion and loving kindness that inspired the Buddha to remain on Earth after his awakening, to show others the path to enlightenment – a state called 'nirvana-in-this-life'. At the end of his life, he entered parinirvana – 'complete nirvana'. Neither death, nor the afterlife, parinirvana is considered to be a state of non-existence, from which the Buddha would never be reborn.

FOUR STAGES TO NIRVANA

'Enlightenment' suggests sudden insight – 'seeing the light' – but in fact reaching nirvana often takes many years. It involves cultivating prajna, or wisdom. This is achieved through meditation, which may act as a catalyst to enlightenment in bringing about sudden flashes of insight.

The Buddha named four stages on the path to nirvana, each of which is marked by release from some of the 'ten fetters' – obstacles to enlightenment. These stages are as follows:

1 **'Stream-enterer'** This first, often momentary and powerful experience of selflessness is a sign that one has overcome the first three fetters. These impediments to enlightenment are the belief that the self is permanent and unchanging; residual doubt in the Buddha's teachings; and the clinging to pointless practices and rituals. Rapture and relief follow when the disciple has understood the nature of 'non-self'.

2 **'Once-returner'** Renewed efforts to weaken the fetters of sensual desire and overcome ill will, aided by the practice of advanced meditation techniques, result in a second, clearer experience of selflessness. At this stage, there is only one rebirth to endure before a disciple attains nirvana.

Above Miroku Bosatsu is the Japanese Maitreya, the future Buddha. Some believe that far into the future he will appear on Earth to save those who have been unable to achieve enlightenment.

3 **'Never-returner'** Complete removal of the first five fetters brings about contentment and loss of desire and a third experience of 'non-self'. 'Never-returners' are reborn into the highest planes of the Sphere of Form.

4 **Arhat** Those who release the last five fetters – craving for material and non-material existence, conceit, restlessness and ignorance – understand the Four Noble Truths and attain enlightenment.

SANSKRIT WORDS

bodhi wisdom, intuition, enlightenment, awakening.

buddha meaning 'awakened', a buddha is any being who has achieved enlightenment (*bodhi*).

mantra a word or phrase with a powerful meaning used as an aid to meditation and as an incantation.

nirvana 'extinction', liberation from the cyclical existence in samsara, or death and rebirth, enlightenment.

parinirvana 'complete nirvana', the nirvana that takes place after death, the complete extinction of the individual, characterized by freedom from the effects of karma.

samadhi a practice in meditation in which one becomes absorbed in the object of meditation, leading to 'one-pointed' concentration.

satori a usually sudden spiritual awakening, an intuitive understanding of the nature of reality, achieved in Zen Buddhism.

vipassana literally 'inward vision' (the Sanskrit term is *vipashyana*), meditation techniques to promote a clear understanding of the nature of reality through insight.

DEVOTION

THE BUDDHA'S DISCIPLES ELEVATED MEDITATION AND OBSERVANCE OF THE RULES ABOVE RITES AND WORSHIP, BUT LATER SCHOOLS ENCOURAGED DEVOTION TO BUDDHAS AND ARHATS. TODAY, RITUAL AND DEVOTION ARE A VALUED PART OF BUDDHIST PRACTICE.

The Buddha warned his first followers against starting a personality cult when he was no longer with them. Their task was to seek out and follow the path that led to spiritual awakening, and his role was to guide them along this path. It was his teaching that was important, not his personality. His life was relevant, but only inasmuch as it acted as an inspiration to others and exemplified the route that everyone's life must take if they are to succeed in achieving spiritual transformation and enlightenment.

Below Circumambulation is an important part of Buddhist devotion. Followers walk around a stupa, statue or shrine reciting mantras or sutras, or meditating.

A FIGURE OF WORSHIP
Despite his wishes to the contrary, within 100 years of his parinirvana, the Buddha was being glorified, not as the one god, creator of the world, as in other religions, but as a superhuman. In addition, Buddhism had adopted a complex pantheon of supernatural beings, and had become more of a religion than a philosophy.

This change was due partly to the popularity of the Mahayana tradition, which emerged during the 1st century CE, and held that faith in the compassion of bodhisattvas, rather than personal effort through meditation and careful observance of the rules of the Sangha, was the key to salvation. However, the Buddha never rejected the beliefs and practices

Above A lay follower washes a statue of the Bodhisattva Jizo at a temple in Japan. Buddhist devotion includes cleaning and caring for public and private shrines and sacred objects.

of older religions, and neither did the Buddhism that followed him. Further, as the early, more intellectually rigorous Buddhism began to reach out to a wider public, the enthusiasm of that public naturally embraced its spirituality.

The early Sangha laid great emphasis on remembrance of the Buddha and on his 'living presence' in stupas that contained his relics. Disciples reported that when they approached these stupas, they observed magical light rays or even the form of the Buddha himself emanating from the stupas. Visions like these inspired followers to make images and venerate them – as representations of the Buddha, not as deities. To invoke the Buddha's 'living presence', images were engraved with sacred words, and small relics, or mandalas, were secreted inside or beneath them.

BUDDHIST PRAYER
In the Theravada tradition, which claims to follow the Buddha's original teachings, prayer was

PROSTRATION

Lay Buddhists and monks perform prostrations as an act of veneration to the Buddha, his teachings and the Sangha, which are collectively called the Three Treasures or the Triple Gem. Prostrations are believed to cleanse the spirit of pride, suppress desire, and clear the mind of *kleshas* – poisonous emotions such as hatred, desires such as lust, and negative attitudes such as laziness – which impede concentration, so Buddhists prostrate themselves before and after meditation. The prostration practices of the different traditions and schools vary: Zen Buddhists often make half-prostrations; in Theravada Buddhism, three 'five-point prostrations' may be performed at the start of puja (worship): palms, elbows, toes, knees and forehead all touch the floor; Vajrayana Buddhists prostrate themselves fully, usually on a mat placed on the floor, with the arms held out in front. Beads may be used to count 108 full-length prostrations made while reciting prayers or mantras.

Right A Thai monk makes a five-point prostration before a statue of the Buddha at Wat Phra Si Ratana Mahathat, a temple in Phitsanulok, Thailand. In the Theravada tradition, prostration is the most respectful form of worship.

secondary to meditation and studying or chanting the scriptures. The role of all these practices was to concentrate the mind, and prayer involved repeating expressions of universal hope – 'May all beings have happiness and the causes of happiness...' – or of veneration for the Buddha. However, Mahayana monks introduced the practice of praying to bodhisattvas and other deities for personal help. Some schools promoted the chanting of mantras, mystical sayings such as *Om mani padme hum* ('Praise to the jewel in the lotus'), as a prayer-like practice to aid concentration.

All traditions consider it meritorious to worship anything that recalls the Buddha or Dharma, to keep a shrine clean and to decorate it with coverings, artworks and lights, and to pay respect to an image that recalls the Buddha or a bodhisattva by reverential gestures and prostrations.

At home, Buddhists set aside a corner for a household shrine, furnished with a statue of the Buddha, or a painting or mandala, where they can retire to study sacred texts, meditate and pray.

Above Buddhists leave offerings of water and even food at a shrine, as well as incense and candles. Placing her hands together in anjali *mudra, the gesture of offering, this woman recites a mantra to aid concentration, or says a prayer.*

BUDDHIST ETHICS

THE DHARMA, THE UNIVERSAL LAW THAT GOVERNS THE MORAL ORDER OF THE UNIVERSE, IS THE WELLSPRING OF BUDDHISM'S ETHICAL TEACHINGS. TODAY, SCRIPTURES THAT TOUCH ON ETHICS ARE BEING RE-EXAMINED TO FIND STANDPOINTS ON NEW MORAL DILEMMAS.

In light of samsara, the doctrine of rebirth, and *ahimsa*, the doctrine of non-violence, where does Buddhism stand on issues such as abortion, embryo research, war and euthanasia?

There is no Buddhist pope, no central authority to rule on ethical issues, so different traditions, schools and individuals have opposing standpoints on many important questions. Few ethical issues are clear-cut. Buddhists are enjoined to cause no harm to living beings, so it would seem that all would oppose animal experiments. However, in the absence of a ruling body, there is no all-encompassing 'Buddhist policy' on such matters.

Above Buddhist monks march for peace in Russia in front of the State Duma in Moscow. Buddhists oppose war and all forms of violence but are having to rethink their stance on such issues as pacifism and the use of force.

CONCEPTION AND BIRTH

Ancient texts clearly conclude that life begins at conception. The general view among Buddhists is that fertilization is the start of life. In countries where Buddhism is the state religion, abortion is banned; where Buddhism predominates but is not the state religion, the practice is permitted. In Japan, the custom has arisen of invoking the Bodhisattva Jizo, protector of children and expectant mothers, in *mizuko kuyo* memorial services for aborted (as well as for miscarried) children.

Stem cell extraction and human embryo cloning for therapeutic purposes are generally supported in countries where Buddhists are a majority or where Buddhism is the state religion. Individuals have expressed the view that these do not infringe the First Precept, which prohibits the taking of life, and are in keeping with the doctrine of samsara.

Left The Bodhisattva Jizo, patron of the oppressed or dying, the Japanese version of the Bodhisattva Ksitigarbha. The statues are sometimes given adornments, and this figure has been adapted to represent pregnant women and unborn children.

THE ENVIRONMENT

The Buddha opposed animal sacrifice and refrained from killing animals and even from harming plants and seeds. He enshrined non-violence toward all living things in the First Precept and banned his followers from professions that harm animals. He recognized the value of the wilderness by retreating to the forest to meditate. Furthermore, Buddhist cosmology suggests that the fate of the physical universe depends on its inhabitants, so that a world occupied by people who failed to protect it would not last as long as one that was cared for by those who lived there.

However, writers on Buddhist ethics conclude that Buddhism's main concern is human progress toward nirvana, not the protection of animals or the ecosystem. Although individuals may be actively involved in such concerns, and they accord with the requirements of the Noble Eightfold Path, Buddhism does not directly address these issues.

Above The Buddhist teachings do not promote environmental protection, but emphasize simple living, non-violence, compassion and loving kindness, and so indirectly encourage environmental concern.

SUICIDE AND EUTHANASIA

The 1960s' incidents of self-immolation by Buddhist monks in protest against religious suppression have left the impression that suicide is sanctioned by Buddhists. At the time, however, there were strong disagreements about the 1960s' incidents, and the current controversy about suicide and euthanasia extends to the Buddhist community.

Many Buddhists regard suicide as contrary to the Dharma teachings on non-violence and a squandering of the opportunity for enlightenment offered by human existence. Academics who have studied the origins of self-immolation and suicide in Eastern societies have discovered that these practices pre-date the introduction there of Buddhism. The Buddhist canon reveals little evidence that the Buddha sanctioned or condoned suicide. Furthermore, the Buddha prohibited suicide or

the assisting of suicide by members of the Sangha in a monastic rule, the Third *Parajika*.

This rule applies equally to euthanasia: causing death intentionally, even out of compassion at the request of someone you love, infringes Buddhist moral teachings.

PEACE

Buddhists and Buddhist organizations have been active in opposing war and terrorism. Yet research has unearthed numerous instances in history when Buddhists have turned to fighting and insurrection.

Damien Keown, a writer on Buddhist ethics, distinguishes between warfare, implying aggression and the intention to kill, and force, which might be applied without aggression – for example, by oppressed Buddhists demanding the right to practise their religion. Warfare changed radically during the 20th century and Keown suggests that, while opposing warfare accords with Dharma teachings, Buddhist thinkers could review their religious stance on pacifism, self-defence, terrorism and concepts such as 'just war'.

Right Tibetans practise prostrations in the presence of the Chinese authorities at the Jokhang temple in Lhasa.

BUDDHISM AND PACIFICISM

THROUGHOUT BUDDHISM'S LONG HISTORY, BUDDHISTS HAVE HAD TO FIND WAYS OF RESISTING LAWS THAT WOULD SUPPRESS THEIR RELIGION AND DESTROY THE SANGHA. PACIFISM HAS BEEN THE ROUTE FOR SOME, PASSIVE RESISTANCE THE WAY FOR OTHERS.

Above A fragment of an inscription of one of the edicts of the 3rd-century BCE Mauryan emperor Ashoka, who proclaimed his support of the Dharma and a change of policy to peaceful co-existence with neighbouring states.

Buddhist doctrine firmly opposes violence. The Dharma teaches that aggression stems partly from a misguided belief that the self is real and needs protection from others. Patience and forbearance are thought to be the correct responses to threat, and compassionate analysis of the situation the only rational response to aggression.

Below In September 2007, monks all over Burma (Myanmar) marched in passive protest against the people's oppression and poverty, brought about by the policies of the military junta.

During the 3rd century BCE, there arose in India a Mauryan ruler who became an icon of pacifism. In 268BCE, Emperor Ashoka of the Mauryan dynasty fought his brothers for the dynastic throne, then set out to conquer what became a vast empire. A bloody war to overthrow Kalinga (modern Orissa), caused a watershed in Ashoka's life. Stricken with remorse at the destruction he had caused, he became a devout lay Buddhist and adopted a policy of complete non-violence. He then dedicated his life to spreading Buddhism throughout his empire.

MODERN CONFLICTS

In modern times, many Buddhists have chosen passive resistance as their response to threat and aggression. This is peaceable action to achieve aims through, for example, non-violent protest, acts of non-co-operation and disobedience, lobbying, or media publicity.

The stance of Tibetan exiles in 1951 against the Chinese occupation of their country is the outstanding example of Buddhist passive resistance to religious repression. The resistance is led by the 14th Dalai Lama, who was strongly influenced by Mahatma Gandhi's *satyagraha* movement of non-violent opposition to colonial rule in India, and he has formed a Tibetan government-in-exile. Inside Tibet, monks, nuns and lay followers have often used permitted religious activities, such as circumambulating a temple, as occasions for demonstrations against the Chinese authorities.

The shocking suicides of six Vietnamese monks and a nun during the 1960s may be seen as an extreme and highly controversial

form of passive resistance. Their objective was to make a stand against, and draw the world's attention to, the anti-Buddhist policies of the dictator Ngo Dinh Diem, and to request religious equality. The deaths by self-immolation of the first two, older, monks, Thich Quang Duc and Thich Tieu Dieu, were sanctioned by their religious authorities. These acts had a spectacular impact on world opinion, but they were later condemned by many Buddhists as contrary to Buddhist teachings.

DOES IT WORK?

The effectiveness of non-violent protest is questionable. Some people argue, for example, that despite almost half a century of passive resistance by the Dalai Lama and his followers, the Tibetan people are no nearer independence, and although the right to practise their religion has ostensibly been restored, it is nevertheless heavily restricted.

Faced with persistent economic decline and political repression, Buddhists living under repressive regimes feel there may be no alternative to passive resistance — or at least little to lose by it.

Non-violent protests by Buddhists took place in Burma (Myanmar) during 2007. Small-scale, non-religious protests against the removal of fuel subsidies evolved into what has been called the 'saffron revolution', as some 20,000 monks all over the country led protests against the economic distress of the population. Monks, supported by the people, marched, carrying the Buddhist flag, while chanting the words of the Buddha. They refused to administer religious services to the military. Within days, many had been arrested, to face possible torture and death at the hands of government agents.

CONSCIENTIOUS OBJECTORS

The Buddha is said to have warned that warriors who are intent on killing at the moment of their death go to a special hell. The 4th-century scholar-monk Vasubandhu warned that all killing is wrong, even in self-defence, and even for conscripted soldiers. In recent years, many South Korean Buddhists have been imprisoned for declaring themselves conscientious objectors and refusing to report for military service when they were conscripted.

The experiences of Aidan Delgado, an American who enrolled in the army on 9/11, are more widely known. After enlistment, Delgado became a Buddhist. In 2003, his unit was sent to Iraq, and his experiences there motivated him to apply for discharge from the military as a conscientious objector. Meanwhile, his unit was transferred to the notorious Abu Ghraib prison in Baghdad, where he witnessed horrifying cruelty and abuse. After his discharge, he published a book about his experiences and became an anti-war activist.

Right Since conscription began in South Korea, some 10,000 Buddhists have declared themselves conscientious objectors. This is a criminal offence for which the penalty is imprisonment. Military police arrested Private Kang Chol-min, a conscript, in November 2003, for staging a protest against government plans to send troops to Iraq.

CHAPTER 3

EARLY BUDDHISTS

During the first centuries after the Buddha passed away, Buddhism grew from a minor sect into a major religion. Within a year of the Buddha's death, his disciples convened a council to review his words and establish a body of doctrine, then travelled across the Indian subcontinent spreading his teachings. The Buddha had been a pioneer of religious organization, founding the first monastic order, the Sangha, which admitted followers of all castes, and permitting the formation of a women's Sangha.

By the 3rd century BCE, schisms appeared and the Sangha split into two traditions. Those who adhered to the Buddha's original teachings were known as the 'elders'. Today, their tradition is called Theravada, or the 'way of the elders'. Another competing tradition elevated the Buddha to the status of a deity, and emphasized the potential of all beings to attain buddhahood. It is known as Mahayana, or the 'great vehicle', meaning that its adherents view their belief as the way to salvation. Later, a third tradition, Vajrayana, or Tantric, Buddhism, which emphasized the attainment of buddhahood in one lifetime, emerged from Mahayana Buddhism. Today, this tradition, which developed in Tibet after the 7th century, is often called Tibetan Buddhism.

Opposite An 8th-century Chinese silk painting of the Buddha preaching. At the beginning of the first millennium, monks and scholars began to translate Buddhist texts into Chinese, facilitating the transmission of Buddhism to China.

Above A contemporaneous statue of Kanishka, the 2nd-century ruler of the Kushan empire, which extended from Afghanistan into India. Kanishka embraced Buddhism and encouraged its spread into Central Asia.

THE FIRST BUDDHISTS

THE WORK OF PRESERVING THE BUDDHA'S TEACHINGS THROUGH THE ORAL TRADITION GAINED MOMENTUM AFTER THE FIRST BUDDHIST COUNCIL. THE LEADING ARHATS TRANSMITTED THE DHARMA TO THE SANGHA, WHO DISSEMINATED IT WIDELY ACROSS INDIA.

Mahakashyapa, ascetic and disciple, was the force behind the preservation of the Dharma at the First Buddhist Council. Without him, Buddhism might have remained just another minor sect among many. He was the unofficial patriarch, the 'father of the Sangha', for some years until, before passing into nirvana, he handed over the role to another arhat, Ananda.

Below This Tibetan rock painting depicts the Buddha with the 16 arhats. According to Mahayana texts, at the First Buddhist Council they renounced nirvana to devote themselves to relieving suffering by teaching the Dharma.

Ananda, whose ability to memorize was awe-inspiring, was charged with relaying the Buddha's long discourses, including the *Digha Nikaya*, a collection of 34 sutras, or suttas. It is said that he also taught thousands of monks.

THE WOMEN'S ORDER

The Buddha had exhorted his monks to teach "for the welfare of the many". After the First Buddhist Council, the Sangha carried his teachings all over the sub-continent. Among these first disciples were many bhikkhunis, or nuns.

While in Vaishali during the fifth year after his awakening, the Buddha was approached by a

Above Since the time of the Buddha, bhikkhus and bhikkhunis have met twice a month to chant the sacred texts. These Tibetan monks of the Geluk sect chant rhythmically to the accompaniment of cymbals.

party of Sakya women led by his aunt, Mahaprajapati, who asked to join the Sangha. The Buddha refused. The women persisted with their request to found an order of bhikkhunis. Eventually, Ananda, whose gift for resolving disputes the Buddha himself had recognized, intervened. He asked

Right This Chinese Tang dynasty tympanum shows Mahakashyapa and Ananda at the Buddha's side. Each led the Sangha after the Buddha's parinirvana, and both ensured the preservation of the Dharma teachings.

the Buddha whether women could attain nirvana. The Buddha affirmed that they could.

The Buddha is said to have feared that the Sangha would not last if women were admitted. (As many contemporary writers point out, such attitudes may be regarded in the context of strong taboos against women in 3rd millennium BCE India.) The Buddha agreed that a women's Sangha could be founded, but on the condition that the women be subject to extra rules, mainly governing chastity and their subordination to the authority of the monks.

Ananda supported these female disciples, helped them with problems of isolation, rejection and discrimination, taught them the rules of practice, preached the Dharma to them, and encouraged the Buddha to grant them ordination. In time, the women's Sangha flourished.

THE GROWING SANGHA

From the perspective of the 21st century, it can be difficult to appreciate the impact during the 3rd millennium BCE of the Sangha, with its women members, on Indian society and its rigid hierarchy of castes. Monasticism was a form of religious organization pioneered by the Buddha, who imposed certain restrictions on membership – criminals, debtors and runaway slaves were excluded, while any bhikkhus or bhikkhunis guilty of a serious offence, such as violence, sexual misconduct or

theft, were expelled. However, he admitted people from all castes, as well as women, believing that all had the potential to attain nirvana.

Clad in the poorest garb and possessing little, bhikkhus and bhikkhunis travelled the country in pairs or small groups, sleeping and meditating in the forests, approaching villages in the mornings to beg alms. Inspiring respect for their calm friendliness toward people of all castes, they were granted many opportunities to teach the Dharma and gained converts. Thus, the Sangha grew.

CAVE VIHARAS

Caves were natural shelters for the homeless poor in India in the late 3rd millennium BCE, including the bhikkhus and bhikkhunis of the early Sangha. The hills around Rajgir, the ancient capital of Maghada, are studded with caves once used by the Buddha and his followers for meditation or as communal dwellings during rainy seasons. Caves were also used for devotion and for meetings and councils. As converts joined the Sangha, cave settlements were extended to establish more permanent viharas. Where the rock was soft, monks would burrow into cliffs and mountainsides to excavate cave complexes with dwellings, shrines and assembly halls, or build meeting halls and temples in wood. No wooden structures remain, but some 12,000 excavated caves have been discovered on the Indian subcontinent, of which perhaps about 8,000 were created by Buddhists, and the remainder by Jains and adherents of the Brahmanic religions.

Above India's magnificent Ajanta cave temples began as a row of four or five monks' cells cut into an escarpment of the Indhyadri hills in Maharashtra by Buddhist monks during the 2nd century BCE.

THE FIRST BUDDHIST SCRIPTURES

THE TEACHINGS OF THE BUDDHA WERE TRANSMITTED BY WORD OF MOUTH FOR SOME 300 YEARS. ACCORDING TO TRADITION, THEY WERE FIRST WRITTEN DOWN DURING THE 1ST CENTURY BCE BY MONKS WORKING IN A CAVE VIHARA, OR TEMPLE, IN SRI LANKA.

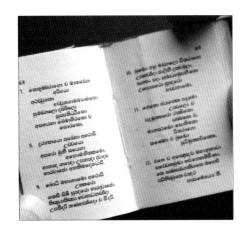

Above Pali, a literary and liturgical language, is written in a number of different scripts. The entire Tripitaka is printed in the Sinhala script, which originated 2,000 years ago, in this modern miniature book.

What language did the Buddha speak? A man of his social status in northern India would have known Sanskrit, the language of the elite, and Magadhi Prakrit, an ancient form of a language that is still spoken today around Bihar. But Buddhism has no official language, because the Buddha directed that the Dharma should be taught in the languages and dialects the people spoke.

Writing was known in India by the 3rd millennium BCE, but not widely, and the Buddha and

Below This wall in the 11th-century Ananda temple in Bagan, Burma (Myanmar), was painted to teach one of the Jataka Tales, or stories of the Buddha's past lives, from the Khuddaka Nikaya, *a section of the* Sutta Pitaka.

his followers would have been illiterate. The Buddha's teachings were summarized in short verses called sutras, which were memorized by chanting. Writing spread across India from about the 3rd century BCE, but was used mainly in commerce. As the written word became more widespread, parts of the canon may have been written down by monks in northern India, but there is no historical evidence to determine when the sutras, which for centuries had been spread through the oral tradition, first appeared in written form.

THE PALI SCRIPTURES

The earliest surviving complete version of the Buddhist scriptures was written in Pali, a language that some scholars believe may be

THE FIRST BUDDHIST BOOKS

Scholars have been unable to date the texts of the Pali canon because they were written on *ola*, the dried young leaves of the talipot, or fan palm, or the Asian Palmyra palm. The leaves were boiled in salt water, to which turmeric may have been added to preserve them, then dried and polished with a pumice stone. They were cut to a regular size, holes were punched in them, and they were bound with cord.

In a tropical climate, palm-leaf manuscripts were vulnerable to attack by damp and insects, so the text had to be repeatedly copied on to new leaves. The oldest surviving palm-leaf texts date from the 11th century CE, but most were made in the 15th century. In cold mountain regions, Buddhists preserved the texts on strips of birch bark, which they rolled up into scrolls. The oldest of these dates from before the 8th century.

related to old Magadhi. Pali was a literary language used for the writing of Buddhist texts.

Buddhism had reached Sri Lanka during the 3rd century BCE through the oral tradition, and it was strengthened during the reign of the Buddhist King Vattagamani (89–77BCE). Under his patronage, a group of monks at the Aluvihara, a cave vihara near Kandy, embarked on a project to write down the Tripitaka (Pali: Tipitaka), the 'three baskets' of teachings that had been established more than a century earlier at the First Buddhist Council and had subsequently spread across the subcontinent.

Transcribing the Tripitaka would have been carried out by the monks as an act of devotion to earn merit, but scholars query why the task was not undertaken in the Buddhist heartlands in north-eastern India, and why it was carried out by monks in a distant cave vihara and not under the supervision of King Vatta-gamani in one of the great monasteries in his capital, Anuradhapura. It is hoped that in time archaeologists may be able to shed light on such questions.

COMMENTARIES

The Pali canon includes commentaries on the core texts, the original Tripitaka. Accompanying the first part, the *Vinaya Pitaka*, or rules for monks and nuns, are supplementary rules, a commentary on the rules and a detailed analysis. The second part is the *Sutta Pitaka*, a collection of discourses attributed to the Buddha and to his leading disciples, while the third is the *Abhidharma Pitaka*, a compilation of texts on Buddhist philosophy. After the 1st century BCE, there were several revisions of the Tripitaka, of which the last part,

the *Abhidharma Pitaka*, reveals some of the biggest changes, with the inclusion of new works.

Despite the difficulty of dating and authenticating the Tripitaka, it remains respected as a work of authority, a trustworthy account of the Buddha's teachings. Since the 1st century CE, it has been copied and translated, modified and supplemented. However, although the various versions differ in their details, all agree on the essentials of the Dharma.

Above A monk in the Haeinsa temple library in South Korea holds a volume of the Korean translation of the Tripitaka printed from original 13th-century woodblocks.

Below A 19th-century illustration of stories from the life of the Buddha as recorded in the Tripitaka. Here, Siddhartha Gautama is engaged in a sumptuous procession with his retinue.

THE GREAT SCHISM

VAJJI, IN INDIA'S FAR NORTH-EAST, WAS THE WORLD'S FIRST KNOWN REPUBLIC, FORMED BY A CONFEDERATION OF CLANS. AMONG ITS CITIZENS WERE THE BHIKKHUS OF THE MAHAVANA MONASTERY IN THE CAPITAL, VAISHALI, WHO RESISTED THE EARLY SANGHA'S STRICT RULES.

There is a legend that the Buddha first visited Vaishali, the beautiful capital of the prosperous Vajji confederation, during the fifth year after his enlightenment. He did this out of compassion, because the city had been visited by drought and a terrible plague. Torrential rains fell after his arrival, washing away the pestilence. The Buddha then delivered the *Ratana Sutta*, the Discourse on Precious Jewels (Buddha, Dharma and Sangha), to the townspeople, and thousands were converted. He also gave other discourses in Vaishali and established several important rules for the Sangha there.

THE SECOND COUNCIL

Much of our understanding of how early Buddhism developed comes from texts written centuries after the Buddha's death, and they often disagree. However, it is generally accepted that about 100 years after the First Buddhist

Council met at Rajagriha in order to review and memorize the Buddha's teachings following his death, another council was held, this time at Vaishali.

It is recorded that 700 arhats attended this Second Council to consider ten practices being followed by bhikkhus from the Mahavana vihara in Vaishali. These monks were accused of accepting gold and silver from lay followers, something the Buddha had denounced. They had also broken the rules on eating and drinking, by consuming palm wine, going on two alms rounds in order to eat twice, drinking buttermilk after meals, eating after midday and 'carrying salt in a horn', which was thought to infringe an

Above In the mid-3rd century BCE, the emperor Ashoka sponsored this pillar surmounted by a lion sculpture at Vaishali. Although it is sinking into soft ground, the pillar still stands at over 11m (36ft) tall.

injunction against storing food. Minor infringements included using the wrong type of mat, and breaking rules governing relationships with other viharas.

The Council leaders found against the Vajjiputtaka bhikkhus and declared their support for strict observance of the rules established by the Buddha. However, the matter did not end there.

NEW SCHOOLS

The Vajjiputtaka bhikkhus did not accept the censure. They may have regarded themselves as progressive, moving on from what they saw as over-rigorous asceticism. To the *sthavira*, or elders of the Council, the conduct of the Sangha was paramount, and to disobey rules and refuse to atone and conform

Below The Dhamekh stupa at Sarnath is said to mark the spot where the Buddha first revealed the Dharma. It has deep foundations and has endured for more than 2,000 years.

was heresy. The Vajjiputtaka bhikkhus are believed to have left the Council and, sometime in the months or possibly years that followed, to have convened their own council, perhaps to discuss new ideas that disagreed with accepted doctrine.

The Buddha had taught that the pinnacle of spiritual achievement is to attain nirvana by following his path and becoming an arhat. A buddha himself does not have a path to follow. He achieves nirvana by his own spiritual efforts at a time when the world has forgotten the Dharma. Around this time, another group of bhikkhus cast doubts on the spiritual perfection of the arhat, suggesting that a bhikkhu might aspire to become a buddha. They called themselves the Mahasamghika, or the 'Great Community'. They remained members of the Sangha, but they set off a wave of new thinking. The group that supported the original teachings became adherents of the Sthaviravada, or 'Teachings of the Elders'.

Below Arhats are ordinary humans who have achieved enlightenment with the help of a buddha. They may reside on Earth to teach the Dharma, but they are not buddhas.

EIGHTEEN SCHOOLS

More and more members of the growing Sangha abandoned the peripatetic life to settle in viharas. Communities developed in isolation, and this, added to the Mahasamghika/ Sthaviravada split and the absence of a central authority, resulted in a sectarian phase of Buddhism, with the emergence of many new schools and sects. Eighteen schools are said to have issued from the orthodox tradition, led by the Sthaviravada school, but in fact there were many more.

One was the Sarvastivada school, which emerged during the 3rd century BCE from the Sthaviravada. Similar to the Mahasamghikas, its adherents doubted the perfection of arhats, but they developed sophisticated theories about *sarvasti*, 'the existence of all things through time'. They believed that the smallest elements of existence, called dharmas, do exist, though they may have a momentary existence; and that they exist in the past and future, as well as the present. These ideas challenge the concept of *anatman*, the idea that there is no self.

Indeed, it has been argued that the Sarvastivadins anticipated some of the findings of modern physics. They believed that nothing we experience is as it appears, and that the universe consists of basic elements of existence. Sarvastivadins thought that such phenomena consisted of combinations of 75 impermanent, interchangeable dharmas – elements such as light, heat, colour, sound, breath, even birth and death.

THE FIRST BUDDHIST STATE

IN THE EIGHTH YEAR OF HIS REIGN, THE EMPEROR ASHOKA TOOK REFUGE IN THE THREE JEWELS, AND SO BECAME THE FIRST BUDDHIST EMPEROR. UNDER HIS COMPASSIONATE RULE, BUDDHISM BECAME THE STATE RELIGION OF INDIA'S MAURYAN EMPIRE.

India's first empire arose during the 4th century BCE, when an obscure prince, Chandragupta Maurya, led a conquering Maghada army westward, beyond the Indus, to overthrow the remnants of Alexander the Great's Greek armies there. His grandson, Ashoka, won the imperial throne in a war against his older brothers in 268BCE and went on to conquer the eastern coastland of Kalinga (southern Orissa) at a staggering cost in resources, lives lost and people displaced. The slaughter is said to have brought Ashoka to a spiritual crisis and, encouraged by a charismatic monk, he embraced Buddhism. Although he kept his armies at combat readiness, and a dictatorial hold on Kalinga, Ashoka pursued peaceful policies.

A BUDDHIST EMPEROR

Ashoka established a state based on practical morality. He issued edicts explaining his understanding of the Dharma – 'Few faults, many good deeds, compassion, giving, truth, purity' – and undertaking that he and his officials would govern and administer justice according to his interpretation of it. He promoted religious tolerance, undertook to protect his people and further their happiness, and used the spoils of his wars to build them dispensaries and reservoirs. He had

Above This engraving shows the emperor Ashoka as an arhat, or enlightened being. He is depicted sitting in the lotus position on a lotus flower, hands in the dhyana mudra. His elongated earlobes and elaborate headdress signify his wisdom and spiritual advancement.

Below The emperor Ashoka's inscription in Brahmi script on this polished stone pillar at Sarnath directs bhikkhus and bhikkhunis not to cause dissension in the Sangha. The upper part of the pillar broke away during a lightning strike.

Below Ashoka's patronage ensured that Indian stone carving continued to evolve after his reign. The four entrance gates, or torana, *to the Sanchi stupa, with their beautiful relief carvings, were added in the 1st century* BCE.

roads built, along which trees were planted and wells dug. He became a vegetarian, discouraged the sacrifice of animals and prohibited animal slaughter on certain days.

ASHOKA'S PILGRIMAGES

Furthermore, Ashoka became an *upasaka*, a lay member of the Sangha, and issued edicts throughout his realm providing moral guidance, rules of conduct and summaries of Buddhist principles. The fact that these edicts did not explain beliefs or philosophy has led to suggestions that political strategy rather than Buddhist morality was behind his policies of religious tolerance, but his long pilgrimages to places associated with the Buddha's life belie this. At Bodhgaya, where the Buddha achieved nirvana, Ashoka had a shrine built, and he erected a stupa over the spot at Kushinara where the Buddha's funeral pyre had burned.

After the Buddha's death, his relics had been divided into eight portions and given to princes who had a claim to them. Each portion was enshrined in a stupa, or burial mound. Ashoka had each set of relics unearthed and split into tiny portions, which were sent all over his empire. Tradition recounts that he had 84,000 stupas built to enshrine them.

PILLAR EDICTS

The emperor's proclamations were inscribed on the bases of soaring stone pillars, which he had erected at pilgrimage sites. Others were engraved on rocks and cave walls across his empire. These edicts, which expounded the

Right The Great Stupa at Sanchi, Madhya Pradesh, originally built during Ashoka's reign, was 7.5m (25ft) high and 18m (59ft) across, but 100 years later it was rebuilt, twice as large.

IMPERIAL ART

Ashoka's patronage of decoration on religious monuments made stone sculpture the preferred medium of Indian artists. Earlier works of art and architecture had been made in wood, and none survive. The polished stone pillars he had erected at holy sites and along pilgrimage routes were surmounted by carved animals, such as lions and bulls, and these represent the pinnacle of this early Indian art form. The famous 2.1m (7ft) high lion capital at Sarnath may be the work of artists trained in the influential Persian sculpture tradition. The four alert lions face the four cardinal directions and once supported a huge carved *Dharmachakra*, or Wheel of the Law. Their feet rest on an abacus bearing images of an elephant, a horse, a bull and a lion, symbolizing the four quarters of the world, interspersed with thousand-spoke wheels. The capital symbolizes Ashoka's role as the *chakravartin*, or Universal King.

Right India's national emblem is the sandstone lion capital that once topped Ashoka's inscribed pillar at Isipatana (now Sarnath). Lightning shattered the pillar, but the lion capital fell 14m (46ft) to the ground unbroken.

Dharma, explained Ashoka's policies, and commemorated his visits to holy places, furthered Buddhism's spread during the 3rd century BCE.

Knowledge of Ashoka's reign faded and was lost until, in the 19th century, archaeologists rediscovered and deciphered Ashoka's rock and pillar edicts. They were inscribed perhaps two centuries before the Buddhist scriptures were written down, so they are the earliest independent evidence for the events and ideas of early Buddhism.

THERAVADA BUDDHISM

THE THERAVADA IS CALLED THE 'SOUTHERN SCHOOL' BECAUSE IT IS THE MAIN BUDDHIST TRADITION IN MANY SOUTH-EAST ASIAN COUNTRIES. IT IS THE OLDEST BRANCH OF BUDDHISM AND CLAIMS TO TRANSMIT THE BUDDHA'S ORIGINAL TEACHINGS.

Ideas and practices that had been condemned as heretical by the Second Buddhist Council in the 4th century BCE flourished in the years that followed, for although the Council headed off major challenges, it failed to calm the intellectual ferment that lay behind them. The Mahasamghika school, for example, went on to develop its idea that bhikkhus and bhikkhunis should aspire to become buddhas, and it spawned many sects, including the Lokottaravada, which taught that buddhas are celestial beings whose appearances and actions on Earth are illusory.

Below Theravada devotees circumambulate the Ruwanveliseya Dagoba in Anuradhapura. Theravada Buddhism emerged in Sri Lanka during the 2nd century BCE, after the emperor Ashoka sent monks of the Vibhajjavada tradition there to teach the Dharma.

NIKAYA BUDDHISM
The Sthaviravada, or 'School of the Elders', held to the teachings of the Buddha, but also spawned sects such as the Dharmaguptaka, which flourished in north-western India around the 1st century CE. Its followers believed that the teachings of a buddha are superior to those of arhats. The Gandharan scriptures, a collection of birch-bark texts that were discovered in Afghanistan and are thought to be part of the Dharmaguptaka canon, are the earliest known Buddhist manuscripts.

The many schools and sects that supported the authority of the Pali canon are known collectively as Nikaya Buddhism. Some were short-lived while others endured for centuries. Some flourished outside India – the Dharmaguptaka, for example, influenced the development of

Above When archaeologists excavated Pataliputra near Patna, the Mauryan capital under Ashoka, they exposed 80 black polished-stone pillars that once supported a great hall – perhaps part of Ashoka's palace, or the vihara where the Third Buddhist Council was held.

Chinese Buddhism. Only one Nikaya Buddhist school remains today, however: the Theravada, or 'Way of the Elders'. The Theravada tradition is believed to have evolved from an orthodox branch of the Sthaviravada called the Vibhajjavada.

THE THIRD COUNCIL
It is thought that a council of arhats may have been held around 250BCE. Theravada sources mention a Third Buddhist Council held at Pataliputra, capital of the Mauryan empire under the emperor Ashoka. Its purpose was to examine unorthodox practices. This was necessary because the emperor's patronage of Buddhist viharas attracted novices for financial rather than vocational reasons. Many falsely claimed to have been ordained, they did not observe the rules and practices of the Sangha, and some were corrupt.

The Council also reviewed unorthodox beliefs, such as the doctrine of *pudgala-vada*, held by

Right The stupa of Sariputra, an arhat considered by the Theravada to be one of the Buddha's leading disciples, rises from the ruins of the later university of Nalanda near Rajagriha. Sariputra was born in a village nearby and entered nirvana at Nalanda.

the Sammitiya sect. Contrary to the Buddha's teaching that there is no soul, no individuality to be reborn, the Sammitiya taught that there must be a 'self' (*pudgala*), an entity capable of accumulating karma and of being reborn. The Buddha taught that the personality is composed of five skandhas, or groups of mental and physical elements. After death, the mental skandhas, freed from physical constraints, are reborn in a new body.

The Council expelled unordained monks and confirmed the Buddha's teachings, declaring unorthodox beliefs, such as *pudgala-vada,* heretical.

THE THERAVADA TODAY

Theravada Buddhists uphold the authority of the Pali canon and believe that they transmit the original teachings and practices of the Buddha and the early Sangha. They revere the historical Buddha, not as an omniscient god but as a man with extraordinary insight and wisdom. They believe that at the end of his life, he passed into final nirvana, beyond the reach of human communication. His life and enlightenment remain as the model for other beings to follow. Those who achieve enlightenment become arhats, but can never be buddhas.

The tradition recognizes the pantheon of past and future buddhas, of whom the Buddha Shakyamuni was one, but not the semi-divine bodhisattvas of the Mahayana schools that arose during the 1st century BCE, nor the idea that beings may be saved

by such celestial beings. Buddhas and arhats teach that beings must save themselves by achieving enlightenment through self-discipline and meditation. This path may take many years and many rebirths.

The Theravada tradition is a strongly monastic one. Working toward enlightenment through strict adherence to rules, studying sacred texts and spending long hours in meditation demands a dedication that only members of a monastic community can afford.

Their support comes from lay followers, who hope to accumulate merit and achieve enlightenment in a future life. Meditation was reserved for monks until the 20th century, when the Theravada reached out to Westerners, who had different expectations.

Below The Theravada Buddhist tradition emphasizes monastic discipline and meditation, rather than faith and prayer to a pantheon of deities, as the path to nirvana. These Theravadan monks are at worship in England.

SPREADING THE DHARMA

THE EMPEROR ASHOKA SENT EMISSARIES TO CARRY THE WORDS OF THE BUDDHA TO EVERY PART OF THE KNOWN WORLD, FROM SOUTH-EAST ASIA TO CHINA AND EVEN EGYPT. BY THE END OF HIS REIGN, BUDDHISM HAD GROWN TO THE STATUS OF A WORLD RELIGION.

Ashoka the Great introduced 50 years of peace and economic prosperity to his empire, which extended from the Himalayas to the Deccan Plateau, and from Assam to Afghanistan. As a Buddhist, he continued to expand his frontiers through peaceful policies, which included supporting Buddhist kings, settling disputes peacefully, road-building, protecting merchants and founding Buddhist viharas.

His policies of religious tolerance and protection benefited both Buddhism and Jainism. Merchants supported these egalitarian religions, and expanding trade encouraged pilgrims to follow the caravans, many of whose routes across India were guarded by Ashoka's armies. In this way, Buddhism spread north-west, beyond Mauryan frontiers.

MISSIONS ABROAD

Ashoka despatched missions far and wide. "[His Majesty] considers victory by Dharma to be the foremost victory", reads his 13th Rock Edict, "And moreover [he] has gained this victory on all his frontiers to a distance of six hundred yojanas" (about 2,500 km/1,500 miles). He sent envoys all over the Hellenistic world, to

Above A Buddha head in the style of the Mon people, early inhabitants of Lower Burma who migrated into Thailand during the 1st millennium CE. The Mon were the first people in South-east Asia to adopt Theravada Buddhism, brought by missionaries from Sri Lanka perhaps as early as the 2nd century BCE.

Syria, Egypt, Macedonia, Cyrene and Epirus. Buddhist communities may have existed around this time in Egypt − scholars have suggested that the monks of the Therapeutae order of Lake Mareotis (now Lake Mariout), outside Alexandria, could have been bhikkhus of the Theravada tradition. Ashoka also sent emissaries to Central Asia and China.

The *Mahavamsa*, an account in the Pali literary language of the kings of Sri Lanka from 543 BCE to 361 CE, tells the story of Ashoka's first and most successful mission − to Sri Lanka. At its head was his son, Mahinda, a bhikkhu, who converted King Devanampiya Tissa to Buddhism on the Mihintale peak. The king supported Ashoka's emissaries in their work of spreading Buddhism in Sri Lanka, and he commissioned the building of the Mahavira monastery for them outside his capital, Anuradhapura. Later,

Below The Dambulla cave vihara in central Sri Lanka was first inhabited by Buddhist monks as early as the 3rd century BCE, when the emperor Ashoka sent his son Mahinda there to teach the Dharma.

Ashoka's daughter, Sanghamitta, brought to Anuradhapura a cutting of the Bodhi tree under the branches of which the Buddha achieved enlightenment. She remained in Sri Lanka, and established a bhikkhuni community.

SPREAD OF THERAVADA

Ashoka's son, Mahinda, belonged to the Vibhajjavada school, a branch of the Sthaviravada school, which recognized the authority of the Pali canon. The Vibhajjavadins rejected the devotional ideas and practices of the new, progressive Buddhist sects. Instead, they emphasized insight based on experience, reasoning and critical analysis. They believed that they transmitted the Buddha's original teachings and referred to themselves as 'the elders' (*thera* in Pali).

By the mid-3rd century BCE, when Mahinda's mission reached Sri Lanka, Vibhajjavada was already beginning to evolve into sub-sects. Mahinda and his missionaries formed a new group, called the Tamraparniya, or 'Sri

Above Pha That Luang, a Buddhist stupa in Vanchang, Laos, and a symbol of the Lao people, is believed to stand on the site of a temple built by Ashoka's emissaries, who arrived bearing relics of the Buddha during the 3rd century BCE.

Lanka Branch'. This was the school that eventually evolved into the Theravada.

Ashoka sent missionaries beyond Sri Lanka, south-east to a land called Suvarnabhumi. Scholars believe that this was part of South-east Asia, close to Sri Lanka, most probably Burma (Myanmar), where the Mon people may have been Buddhist since the 2nd century BCE. They were the link through which Buddhism

was transmitted to the Khmer peoples, who inhabited the lands that are now Thailand, Cambodia and Laos. From Sri Lanka, Buddhism also spread to Vietnam and Indonesia.

Below Ananda temple in Bagan was built by the Mon people in the 11th century CE. One of the best surviving examples of the Mon architectural style, it is covered in stone sculptures depicting events in the life of the Buddha.

Below The Kashmir Valley was part of the Mauryan empire, and after Buddhist missions reached Srinagar, the capital, during the reign of the emperor Ashoka, the region became a centre of Buddhism.

THE VIHARA

SIMPLE SHELTERS FOR WANDERING BHIKKHUS AND BHIKKHUNIS SOON DEVELOPED INTO COMPLEX TEMPLE PRECINCTS WITH MAGNIFICENT MEETING HALLS, SHRINES AND STUPAS. UNIQUE STYLES OF TEMPLE ARCHITECTURE EVOLVED WHEREVER BUDDHISM SPREAD.

Early Buddhist monks lived in huts made of sticks and leaves. In time these evolved into brick and stone structures built around a courtyard, which was used for meetings and teaching. By the 3rd century BCE, some of the larger communities had replaced the open courtyard with a meeting hall. Shrines, image halls and buildings for special purposes, such as bath houses, soon followed, and the term 'vihara' ('dwelling'), expanded its original meaning to embrace the monastery complex.

THE FIRST VIHARA

Only the stone foundations remain at the site of Jetavana, the first Buddhist vihara, which was built in a grove near the large city of Shravasti by a rich merchant, Anathapindika, as a rainy season retreat for the Buddha and his followers. By the 7th century CE, Jetavana had grown into a large community with separate cells and courtyards for bhikkhus and bhikkhunis, refectories, wells, wash-houses, a dispensary and a library, as well as meeting halls and shrines.

Missionary bhikkhus and bhikkhunis established viharas outside towns on trade routes near people, who would give material support, but remote enough to allow peace and solitude for meditation. Jetavana provided the model for these and for the later viharas established outside India. Like Jetavana, many were financed by wealthy business people and supported by local rulers.

Ideally, a vihara occupied a pleasant spot on a hill, sheltered or shaded by trees and near an abundant water supply. It had properly constructed buildings for different uses, and separate dwellings for bhikkhus and bhikkhunis. From early in the 1st millennium CE, viharas were built

Above Distinctive architectural styles appeared in the Buddhist regions surrounding India. Wat Arun in Bangkok, Thailand, has a tall prang, or tower, a feature adopted from buildings of the Khmer, who once ruled Siam.

on hills and mountains across Asia, from Persia in the west to China, Korea and Japan in the east.

TEMPLES OF THE EAST

The decorative temples of the Mahayana sects of East Asia, with their curving roofs and overhanging eaves supported on rows of columns and complex bracketing, seem almost to epitomize Buddhist architecture. In fact, they were derived from the Chinese tradition of palace-building, and the pagoda – the East Asian form of the Indian stupa – derives from the traditional palace gatehouse. Few remain in China today, but the

Left Tibet's Ganden Namgyeling was built on a mountain top outside Lhasa in 1409 by Tsongkhapa, one of the most learned commentators on the scriptures. Ganden became a notable Tibetan Buddhist university.

Right Wat Naung Khan, Kengtung, built in brick and stucco and heavily gilded, has the stepped roofs that are characteristic of Burmese architecture. The distinctive stupa evolved from the Sri Lankan dagoba.

style was faithfully copied in Japan, where some of the early temples are among the world's oldest wooden buildings.

In China, Korea and Japan, a vihara is traditionally a walled compound surrounding a number of separate buildings, all of which face south, the direction of light and growth. In addition to the monks' residences, a library and hall for lectures and meditation, there are traditionally several shrine halls devoted to the Buddha and to deities, such as Guanyin, the Bodhisattva of Compassion, where offerings are made. Inside, images are arrayed on a platform, like emperors enthroned in their audience halls. There may be a pagoda in the centre of the complex, enshrining relics and other sacred objects.

Below A belfry is traditionally sited on the north side of a temple compound. The bell is struck before ceremonies, to ward off evil spirits. This ancient bronze bell is in the Hwagyesa temple in Seoul.

Many storeys symbolize the sacred status of the pagoda, for at this time only the palaces of emperors had multiple roofs. There may also be a belfry and a drum for summoning practitioners for devotion.

Viharas became increasingly large and powerful, housing thousands of monks, owning vast areas of land and possessing art treasures. Some, such as Nalanda, India's great Buddhist university, became respected teaching institutions.

CHAITYAGRIHAS

Caves that served as temporary accommodation for wandering bhikkhus were expanded into cave viharas as the Sangha grew into more settled communities. A shrine hall was soon added, often with a stupa built into one end. In western India, these Buddhist stupa halls, or *chaityagrihas*, were carved out of rocky cliffs and hillsides on a monumental scale. Those at Bhaja and Karla in Maharashtra were excavated during the 1st century BCE.

The *chaityagriha* evolved into the great Indian architectural tradition of rock-cut temples, of which Ellora in Maharashtra is the outstanding example. The first 12 of Ellora's 34 cave temples were excavated by Buddhists and the remainder by Hindus and Jains. In a spirit of co-operation, followers of different religions in ancient India would often occupy the same temple site.

Right Cave 10 at Ellora is called the Carpenter's Cave because its roof is carved to simulate the curved wooden ribs of an early Buddhist temple. The Buddha statue sits before a 10m (33ft)-high stupa. This magnificent chaityagriha dates from 600–800CE.

THE MONASTIC COMMUNITY

THERAVADA BHIKKHUS AND BHIKKHUNIS MUST MEDITATE AT DAWN, NOON AND SUNSET, AND DEPEND ON DONATIONS FOR FOOD AND CLOTHING. MORE THAN 200 RULES GOVERN EVERY ASPECT OF THEIR DAILY LIFE, FROM EATING TIMES TO BEHAVIOUR AND ETIQUETTE.

Theravada Buddhists accept that to attain nirvana requires rigorous discipline to improve self-awareness and long hours spent in meditation. Traditionally, lay devotees, especially those with families, accept that they may not achieve enlightenment in their current life. Instead, they make it their goal to be reborn into a state of existence from which they may attain nirvana in the next life. They try to accumulate merit by cultivating virtues and by obeying the Five Precepts: not to take life, not to steal or lie, not to take part in inappropriate sexual activity,

Below Monks and nuns gain wisdom and understanding from modern technology as well as from ancient texts. Many log on to the Journal of Buddhist Ethics, *a website offering articles and discussion groups.*

and not to use intoxicants. They study the Dharma and support the Sangha by donating food, robes and even medicines.

PRECEPTS AND RULES

All bhikkhus and bhikkhunis, from novices to vihara leaders, must obey ten precepts. In addition to the basic five observed by all Buddhists, they must not eat after midday, attend public entertainments, ornament themselves or use perfumes, sleep in a 'high' (luxurious) bed, or handle 'gold or silver' (money).

When they join a vihara, they must shave their heads as a mark of renunciation, and wear monastic dress. They cannot earn money to support themselves, but must depend on lay followers to provide the necessities of life. That means eating whatever they are

Above Bhikkhus accept robes donated by the laity on Kathina Day after the rainy season retreat. All must follow special rules governing their daily lives.

given (including meat, as long as it was not killed especially for them), and wearing robes made from fabric donated by the laity.

CODE OF CONDUCT

Lay devotees may also observe more precepts on holy days, when they visit a vihara to meditate and hear talks on the Dharma. Teaching is an important part of the relationship between monks, nuns and lay followers.

OBSERVANCE DAYS

Buddhist monks and nuns have always gathered on new and full moon days – and some also on quarter moon days – to recite the *Pratimoksa*. During this ceremony, called the *posadha* (Pali: *uposatha*), bhikkhus and bhikkhunis confess to each other their infringements of the rules. Any item or privilege gained by breaking a rule must be forfeited.

Monks teach the Dharma on *posadha* days to lay devotees, who attend the viharas to hear talks, join in the meditation and sometimes also in the recitation of the rules.

Five of the year's 12 full-moon days are occasions for special celebration. New Year is one and another is Vesak, or Buddha Day, which takes place on the first full-moon day in May or June, and is held to celebrate the Buddha's birth, enlightenment and parinirvana. Magha Puja, or Sangha Day, in March commemorates the Buddha's delivery of rules for the Sangha, the *Ovada Patimokkha*.

Bhikkhus and bhikkhunis must also follow the sets of rules laid down in the *Vinaya Pitaka*, the first part of the Pali canon. The *Vinaya* begins with the code of conduct, or *Pratimoksa* (Pali: *Pratimokkha*), and it usefully provides a case study on how and why each rule in the code came to be adopted. Many of these rules, which cover dress and comportment toward other members of the Sangha, in addition to rules governing serious moral issues, are obsolete, but the *Parajika* dharmas, or offences that merit expulsion, are enforced. They prohibit killing or inciting others to kill, stealing, all sexual activity, and falsely claiming to have attained superior states of consciousness. Any bhikkhu or bhikkhuni who commits one of these offences is considered 'defeated', and will be expelled from the Sangha.

The *Pratimoksa* has changed since it was written down in the 1st century BCE. In the versions of different traditions and schools, the number of rules ranges from 218 to 263 for bhikkhus and 279 to 380 for bhikkhunis.

Every minute in the life of every bhikkhu and bhikkhuni is structured by rules. They must rise

Above The Buddha taught his followers to probe and question the teachings. This picture shows Tibetan monks debating points of doctrine in the meditation hall of the Kopan vihara in Kathmandu, Nepal.

before dawn, meditate before making their alms round and eat before noon. They must study and teach, observe the twice-monthly holy days and make a retreat for three months every year. Through these rules, their life becomes a preparation and training for attaining enlightenment.

Below Theravada monks meditate in Luang Prabang, Laos. Monks and nuns spend several hours a day meditating as part of their monastic discipline.

BUDDHIST TERMS

Cosmic Buddha In Mahayana Buddhism, the compassionate buddha who is eternally omnipresent and a fount of spiritual sustenance. In esoteric Buddhism, the Cosmic Buddha is represented as Vairocana, the personification of the truth of the universe and of wisdom.

Pitaka A Pali word meaning, literally, 'basket'. The canon of Buddhist scriptures, which consist of the Tripitaka ('three baskets'): the *Vinaya Pitaka*, the *Sutta Pitaka* and the *Abhidharma Pitaka*.

Pratimoksa (Pali: *Pratimokkha*) Part of the Pali canon that lays out rules of conduct both for Buddhist monks and nuns as well as for lay followers.

Sunyata The concept that all phenomena are empty of any unchanging reality.

Sutra (Pali: 'sutta') Short verses that summarize the Buddha's teaching, and that are memorized by chanting.

THE MAHAYANA

NEW INTERPRETATIONS OF THE BUDDHA'S TEACHINGS EMERGED FROM THE MANY SCHOOLS AND SECTS THAT AROSE DURING THE CENTURIES FOLLOWING HIS DEATH. THEY CRYSTALLIZED IN THE TEACHINGS OF THE MAHAYANA TRADITION, WHICH SURVIVES TODAY.

Above In Mathura, south of Delhi, the Mahayana tradition influenced a style of delicate and realistic art and sculpture. It reached its apogee in the Gupta school around the 5th century CE, which was when this pink sandstone head was carved.

By the 3rd century BCE, the events of the Buddha's life had become interwoven with myth, and he seemed almost divine. The arhats whom he had guided to enlightenment taught that on his death, he passed into parinirvana, a realm out of reach of human contact. However, later generations challenged this teaching, and bold new philosophical ideas developed, including the belief that the Buddha is everywhere and ever-present.

THE 'COSMIC' BUDDHA

One of these schools was the Mahayana, which emerged in the 1st century BCE. Its adherents saw the Buddha as supremely powerful, omniscient and omni-present – that is, all-seeing and eternally present to give spiritual help to his devotees.

This conception of the 'cosmic' Buddha owes something to the ideas of early schools, such as the Mahasamghika, which believed that the Buddha lived and died as a man, but was in fact a celestial being who had suffered rebirth to teach earthly beings the way to enlightenment. However, modern scholars do not accept that the Mahayana school evolved from any single school. Some experts think it developed as an intellectual tradition within the Sangha over several centuries.

During the 1st millennium CE, the Mahayana, with its radical ideas about buddhahood, grew to rival the Theravada in the size of its following. It came to be called the Eastern tradition, because pilgrims carried it to Central Asia, China, Korea, Japan, Tibet and Mongolia, where it took root,

Left This detail from a 13th-century Japanese hanging scroll mandala, made of silk and gold, shows Vairocana surrounded by mythical buddhas of the four cardinal directions and the four greatest bodhisattvas.

THE 'GREAT VEHICLE'

So central to Mahayana teachings was the bodhisattva ideal that for many years the school was known as the Bodhisattvayana, or 'Bodhisattva Way'.

It called itself 'Mahayana', a Sanskrit word meaning 'great way', or 'great vehicle', because its founders believed they had understood the truth of the Buddha's message – that personal enlightenment attained without the enlightenment of others was not true enlightenment – and discovered the only way to salvation from samsara. They disparaged the schools that preceded them, led by the Theravada, as 'Hinayana', meaning 'lesser way', or 'lesser vehicle' – implying that their adherents could see only part of the picture, so their ideas were imperfect.

Above The early caves at Ajanta were carved by bhikkhus of the Sravakayana, who depicted the Buddha's past lives in wall paintings. Centuries later, Mahayana communities enlarged the site and painted more images.

Theravada and Mahayana evolved as separate traditions within the Sangha, but both acknowledged as their foundation the Buddha's teachings preserved in the Pali canon. They also shared universities and even viharas, and some modern scholars believe that certain bhikkhus and bhikkhunis may have accepted teachings of both traditions. The Mahayana, however, went on to develop its own canon. Today, the doctrinal differences between the Mahayana and Theravada traditions continue to exist.

merged with local beliefs, myths, deities and religious practices, and eventually flourished.

In fact, the strongest appeal of the Mahayana was as the devotional branch of Buddhism, and to the laity, rather than to Sangha intellectuals. By making offerings of flowers (symbols of impermanence), candles (symbols of enlightenment) and incense (symbol of the spread of the Dharma) at shrines, while chanting sutras or making prostrations or circumambulations, lay followers could invoke the intercession of a buddha or a bodhisattva for salvation. Significantly, however, Mahayana Buddhists supplicate buddhas and bodhisattvas not for personal enlightenment and release from samsara, but rather for the salvation of all beings.

THE BODHISATTVA IDEAL

The traditional belief had been that the Buddha was a bodhisattva until his awakening: a being destined to become a buddha, but who, on enlightenment, did not enter parinirvana, but instead remained on Earth to show others the path to salvation. But both the Buddha and the Elders who led the Sangha after his death taught that few beings are destined to become buddhas. The goal of human existence is to achieve enlightenment and so become an arhat and enter nirvana.

The Mahayana regarded this ideal of the Elders as fundamentally selfish. Arhats, they argued, turn their backs on suffering humanity in order to achieve personal salvation. Mahayana intellectuals considered arhats inferior to bodhisattvas, whose role they exalted as that of saviour of beings trapped in samsara.

The ideal is the bodhisattva: one who works compassionately through many rebirths for the enlightenment of all beings. Mahayana Buddhists believe that everyone can and should aspire to become a bodhisattva and to eventually attain buddhahood.

Above Mahayana bhikkhus spread Buddhism into Central Asia from the 1st century CE – at around the time when the halo may have first appeared in Buddhist art of the region. This 8th-century silk banner was found in the caves at Dunhuang, in modern Gansu province, China.

BODHISATTVAS

MAHAYANA TEACHES THAT EVERY SENTIENT BEING HAS THE POTENTIAL TO BECOME A BUDDHA AND SHOULD STRIVE TO REALIZE IT BY SEEKING SELF-PERFECTION AND FOLLOWING THE PATH TO BUDDHAHOOD. THE FIRST STEP ON THIS PATH IS TO BECOME A BODHISATTVA.

Above The Laughing Buddha is the 6th-century CE Chinese monk Budai, believed to have been an incarnation of the Bodhisattva Maitreya.

When the Buddha told tales of himself as a young man, he described himself as 'an unenlightened bodhisatta', according to the Pali scriptures. Bodhisatta, or 'bodhisattva' in Sanskrit, literally means 'enlightenment being', and was originally a term reserved for the Buddha who, out of compassion for suffering humanity, remained in the world after his awakening to teach the Dharma.

According to the scriptures, the Buddha lived through many lives and deaths, and before his last appearance on Earth had advanced along the path to enlightenment. He might have attained samsara as an arhat, but as a buddha he could pass on knowledge of the way to enlightenment to others. It is believed that eons earlier, he had taken a vow in the presence of a buddha who had lived on Earth in another age to seek perfect wisdom and attain buddhahood.

Below Wenshu, China's Mañjushri, lives on the sacred Mount Wutai in Shanxi, where he first appeared in China. Pilgrims to the Pusading temple on one of the mountain's five peaks have included two Qing emperors.

During its most formative years, between 100BCE and 100CE, the Mahayana reinterpreted the concept of the bodhisattva and elevated it to an ideal. In Mahayana Buddhism, any being may consciously set out on the path to buddhahood. At some point, a bodhisattva attains a mental state called *bodhicitta* ('enlightenment mind'). This is the motivation or decision to become enlightened – but not for personal salvation.

The 'enlightenment mind' possesses infinite compassion and seeks salvation for all other sentient beings. To this end, a bodhisattva takes a vow to help others along the path to enlightenment through as many lifetimes as it takes. Bodhisattvas can alleviate suffering, teach the Dharma and help other beings to progress along the path to nirvana. They vow to attain enlightenment and pass into nirvana only when all beings have been saved from the burden of samsara.

THE BODHISATTVA PATH

To progress along the path to buddhahood, bodhisattvas must cultivate compassion (*karuna*) and the six *paramitas*, or perfections: generosity (*dana*), morality (*sila*), patience (*kshanti*), diligence (*virya*), concentration (dhyana) and insight (prajna). *Upaya*, or 'skilful means' – the crucial ability to teach in a way that is perfectly adapted for those who receive the knowledge – is a later addition to the list, along with *pranidhana*, or

conviction of the rightness of the path, *bala paramita*, or spiritual strength, and *jñana paramita*, or perfect knowledge.

CELESTIAL BUDDHAS AND BODHISATTVAS

On reaching the seventh stage, or *bhumi*, along this path, bodhisattvas attain supernatural powers. They can instantly appear anywhere, for example. However, of the many bodhisattvas, only four have reached this stage. They are the celestial bodhisattvas, who have the powers of spirits and the insights of fully enlightened beings, so they have miraculous abilities to help beings lost in suffering.

The supreme bodhisattva of compassion, and foremost of the bodhisattvas, Avalokiteshvara, protects followers from the Four Great Perils – shipwrecks, wrongful imprisonment, theft and fire – and from lions, poisonous snakes, wild elephants and disease. He is depicted in many different forms – holding a lotus, bearing water, descending from heaven on a lotus, with 11 heads symbolizing the 11 virtues with which he conquers the 11 desires that impede enlightenment, and multiple arms, signifying the many powers that he uses to help the suffering.

Maitreya is the only bodhisattva who waits in the Tushita heaven for the end of the period of the Buddhist Law, when the Buddha Shakyamuni's teachings are forgotten. Then he will descend to Earth as the new buddha, to illuminate the world with the truths about suffering and existence. He is depicted standing, wearing a crown and jewellery, or seated, with one or both feet touching the Earth.

The bodhisattva of wisdom and religious doctrine, Mañjushri is usually shown with a book, the symbol of knowledge, and holding a flaming sword in his right hand, signifying the power of knowledge and wisdom to overcome ignorance. Mañjushri is invoked to improve memory to learn Buddhist

Below Statues of Jizo console the dead in a Tokyo cemetery. Jizo, the Japanese form of Ksitigarbha, protects pilgrims, travellers and children, and is invoked in shrines to commemorate aborted children. Ksitigarbha is also known as Sai-snying-po (in Tibet) and Dizang (in China).

texts. The Chinese believe that the Buddha created Wenshu, their name for Mañjushri, to bring his teachings to them, in order to save them from spiritual ignorance.

The bodhisattva of the dying and the oppressed, and overlord of the ten kings of hell and the six realms of rebirth of the Buddhist universe, Ksitigarbha vowed to release all beings from the torments of hell. He is depicted seated on a lotus, crowned, holding the sacred jewel of Buddhism in his right hand and making the gesture of giving, the *vadara* mudra, with his left, or dressed as a monk descending into the flames of hell to rescue sufferers.

Left Tara is the female form of Avalokiteshvara, foremost of the bodhisattvas. This dynamic Tibetan Drolma, or Green Tara, sits with her right leg extended, indicating her readiness to leap into action to save others. Avalokiteshvara is known as Chenrezi in Tibet, Guanyin (female) in China and Kannon in Japan.

THE TEN *BHUMIS*

Cultivating the *paramitas*, or self-perfection, enables a bodhisattva to progress through ten stages, or *bhumis*, of spiritual growth. Those who reach the final stages may elect to become a buddha. The ten *bhumis* are:

1 **Joy** – accompanies *dana*, giving, or generosity.
2 **Purity** – results from perfecting *sila*, or morality.
3 **Shining light** – is the consequence of mastering *kshanti*, or patience.
4 **Brilliance or radiance** – results from persevering in *virya*, or diligence.
5 **Invincibility, the overcoming of illusions** – the result of attaining the higher stages of dhyana, or concentration.
6 **Supreme wisdom** – follows the attainment of prajna, or insight.
7 **Far-advanced** – the effect of mastering *upaya*, or skilful means.
8 **Immobility** – the effect of *pranidhana*, or conviction in the rightness of the path.
9 **Spiritual intelligence** – accompanies *bala paramita*, or spiritual strength.
10 **Dharma cloud** – the power to end afflictions caused by ignorance is the reward of *jñana paramita*, or perfect knowledge.

THE SANSKRIT SCRIPTURES

AROUND THE 1ST CENTURY BCE, WHEN THERAVADA MONKS IN SRI LANKA WERE WRITING DOWN THE PALI SCRIPTURES, NEW TEXTS APPEARED IN INDIA AMONG MAHAYANA FOLLOWERS. THEY WERE WRITTEN IN SANSKRIT, THE LANGUAGE OF THE ELITE AND EDUCATED.

Like the Pali scriptures, the Mahayana texts were written in sutras, or short verses. They were said to represent the words of the Buddha, but they were not the old, familiar teachings that had been learned and chanted by generations of monks. They were new texts, written anonymously, and their origins remain mysterious.

THE PERFECTION OF WISDOM

Among the earliest Mahayana scriptures are the *Prajñaparamita*, or Perfection of Wisdom sutras, which may first have been written as early as 100BCE, but which appeared in revised versions over the following four centuries.

These include the popular short *Diamond Sutra*, which elaborates on ways to cut through the mental attachments and illusions that bind the mind to samsara; and the *Heart Sutra*, which describes the bodhisattva Avalokiteshvara's insight into the fundamental emptiness of all phenomena.

The *Prajñaparamita* literature enlarges on the idea of attaining wisdom (prajna) as a means of release from existence. The texts introduce the ideal of the compassionate bodhisattva and the perfections (*paramitas*) the bodhisattva must achieve in order to attain Perfect Buddhahood. The Mahayana emphasis on the bodhisattva first appears in this

Above Mahayana sutras were written in Sanskrit, which was the language of philosophy and literature in ancient India. Sanskrit brought Buddhist ideas into mainstream Indian thought.

literature, which exhorts and inspires Dharma followers to walk the bodhisattva path to the perfection of wisdom for the sake of other beings.

THE LOTUS SUTRA

The term 'Mahayana' first appears in the text of the *Sutra on the White Lotus of the True Law*. This sutra, presented as a discourse the Buddha delivered late in his life to a large assembly at Vulture Peak, outside Rajagriha, introduced many ideas that opposed traditional Buddhist teachings. It portrayed the Buddha as a being who had achieved nirvana eons before his appearance on Earth to teach the Dharma to beings lost in samsara. It also presented the radical idea that the Buddha did not enter a realm out of reach of spiritual communication but remains spiritually present in the world, perhaps even eternal.

Left The Buddha expounds the Diamond Sutra in the frontispiece to this version, printed from wood blocks on 11 May 868. Found in the Mogao caves, Dunhuang, China, it is the oldest book with a known print date.

THE BUDDHIST TRINITY

The trinity is a common symbol in Buddhist cosmology. For example, there are three types of enlightened being. Arhats (sometimes called *sravakas*) are 'hearers' – they attain enlightenment by following the path shown to them by a buddha. The Buddha Shakyamuni is a *samyaksambuddha* – he attained enlightenment through his own spiritual efforts and remained in the world to teach others. *Pratyekabuddhas* are 'lone buddhas' – they reach enlightenment and enter nirvana without ever teaching the truth to other beings.

The later Mahayana texts describe the Buddha Shakyamuni as having three bodies (*trikaya*), in three dimensions. The *nirmanakaya* is the physical body he inhabited on Earth, which was, nevertheless, capable of miraculous transformations. The *sambhogakaya* is the object of devotion, the heavenly body he inhabits in another plane where he teaches the Dharma to assembled bodhisattvas. The *dharmakaya* is his transcendent body or essence, said to be his 'real' body, which is synonymous with the ultimate truth.

Above The seven-storey Big Wild Goose pagoda of Da Cien temple, Xi'an, was built in the 7th century as a library for texts brought from India by the pilgrim Xuanzang, who spent the rest of his life translating them.

The *Lotus Sutra* is revered in the Far East. Many Sanskrit scriptures did not survive in India after the 1st millennium CE and were preserved in translation in China.

HIDDEN TEACHINGS

Mahayana Buddhists believe the sutras are the Buddha's recorded words. Many Mahayana concepts are reinterpretations of his sayings or actions, and its adherents accept the explanation given in the *Lotus Sutra* that the Buddha had applied 'skilful means' in revealing the Dharma to his followers. He had taught them as much as they could then assimilate, but he had not imparted all of his teachings.

Right Among the treasures of Hemis gompa (vihara) in Ladakh, Tibet, is the Kanjur, the 'Word of the Buddha' Mahayana scriptures in 98 volumes. Wrapped in silk, they are stored on shelves in the library.

More advanced knowledge had been written down and hidden away – the *Lotus Sutra* had been guarded by the Naga King at the bottom of a lake – until the time, some three centuries later, when the Buddhist community was ready to receive them.

Today neither Theravada Buddhists nor Buddhist scholars accept the Mahayana texts as authentic transcripts of the Buddha's words. During the early centuries CE, however, the ideas set forth in these sutras appealed to the spiritual nature of many in India, inspiring enthusiasm and passion. By contrast, the orthodox texts can seem, as one Indian philosopher commented, "a cold, passionless metaphysics devoid of religious teaching".

MAHAYANA PHILOSOPHY

DURING INSIGHT MEDITATION, MAHAYANA MONKS CONTEMPLATED *ANATMAN*, THE NON-SELF, AND THE IMPERMANENCE OF EXISTENCE. THEIR PHILOSOPHY CENTRED ON THE CONCEPT OF *SUNYATA*, OR EMPTINESS, AND CONCLUDED THAT EVERYTHING IS AN ILLUSION.

The *Abhidharma Pitaka*, the third 'basket' of the Pali scriptures, contains knowledge the Buddha considered too profound for most of his disciples. Only Sariputra, his most advanced arhat, possessed the wisdom to understand it.

The compilers of this remarkable scripture collected and clarified the Buddha's teachings on philosophy, metaphysics and phenomena relating to human experience and psychology, and presented them systematically in seven books. These innovative works explore the nature of reality and the factors that give rise to events, and they had a profound effect on Mahayana thought.

One philosophical conundrum the Buddhists of the ancient world tried to solve was the question of identity. Although they accepted that humans and other beings are empty of *atman*, or self, they questioned the idea that everything is empty of self. Some identifiable aspect of a person must surely endure to be reborn?

DHARMAS

The *Abhidharma* examined experience and classified it in terms of dharmas, the smallest, indivisible components of all phenomena in the universe. It identified 82, all but one of which are said to be conditioned: that is, they come into existence as part of the

Above Nagarjuna (2nd century CE) was one of Buddhism's most influential philosophers. This statue of him is at Kagyu Samye Ling monastery and Buddhist centre in Scotland.

Below The doctrine of dependent arising teaches that phenomena arise together in an interdependent net of cause and effect, an idea often expressed by an image of reflections – and reflections of reflections.

network of cause and effect – according to the doctrine of *pratitya-samutpada*, or dependent arising. Nirvana is different; it arises independently.

Dharmas may be thought of as groups of momentary events, rather like the sub-atomic quarks, leptons and other particles of high-energy physics. They are ever-changing, short-lived and travel only in groups. The skandhas that constitute the physical and mental makeup of living beings – body, feeling, perception, character – comprise groups of dharmas, but the fifth skhandha, consciousness, consists of just one.

The *Abhidharma* found an explanation to the conundrum of non-self in dharmas: these fundamental, irreducible components from which all reality is formed must have an own-identity, an unchanging reality.

EMPTINESS

The *Prajñaparamita*, or Perfection of Wisdom sutras, of the 1st century CE probed emptiness, *sunyata*, more deeply. They examined objects, sensations, beings and, eventually, the 82 dharmas, and concluded that all phenomena are devoid of any unchanging reality.

The great Buddhist philosopher of the 2nd century CE, Nagarjuna, supported their conclusions. Since dharmas are phenomena, he argued, in works inspired by the *Prajñaparamita*, they originate from some cause and cannot, therefore, have a fixed identity. They must be devoid of reality.

Sunyata is a disturbing concept because its implications affect everything. What we think of as the ocean, or a bowl, or the mind has no permanent identity because it is composed of groups of changing, impermanent dharmas, which are themselves devoid of identity or reality. Further, if the

Above Nalanda, near Patna, India, was one of the first great universities and the leading centre of Mahayana learning. At its height, some 10,000 students from all over the Eastern world, adherents of myriad schools and sects, studied there.

world and everything in it is made up of dharmas, and dharmas are not real, the world is an illusion.

Every aspect of existence is affected, right back to the Noble Eightfold Path. Right speech and right action stem from an accepted view of right and wrong, but right and wrong are phenomena composed of dharmas and so empty of any reality. "Even nirvana, I say, is like a magical illusion, is like a dream...", concludes the *Prajñaparamita*.

To the modern mind, these complex ideas seem nihilistic, but scholars speculate that they may have originated among Mahayana intellectuals struggling to interpret the *Abhidharma* in the light of the nothingness, the emptiness they

experienced at the higher stages of insight meditation. Attributing identities and realities to objects, people, opinions and ideas, they realized, puts obstacles in the way of seeing things as they are. Our perception of reality is a construction that enables us to understand the world, but distorts our understanding. Liberation is found at the point where identities, interpretations and opinions disappear.

Below The Abhidharma *preserves the early Buddhists' ideas about time. The* khanavada, *or theory of momentariness, says that a dharma arises, exists for a moment, then passes away before the next one arises.*

MAHAYANA SCHOOLS

THE 2ND CENTURY CE INDIAN PHILOSOPHER NAGARJUNA WAS SO INFLUENTIAL THAT HE IS OFTEN CALLED THE 'SECOND BUDDHA'. HIS IDEAS ARE SAID TO HAVE TURNED THE WHEEL OF THE DHARMA, AND THEY INSPIRED THE FORMATION OF NEW MAHAYANA SCHOOLS.

Nagarjuna was probably born into a Brahmin family in Andhra Pradesh, southern India, around 150CE. He became a Buddhist monk and is believed to have studied at a vihara at Nalanda, near modern Patna. The writings attributed to him indicate that he may have supported orthodox beliefs – he seems to have known the *Abhidharma* – but he strongly defended Mahayana ideas.

THE TWO TRUTHS

The 2nd century CE was a time of philosophical exploration in India. Not only did new Buddhist schools continue to emerge – such as the Sautrantaka and the Vatsiputriya, which took opposite views on self and non-self and the effects of dharmas – new Brahminical schools had also appeared, including a Vedic school of logic, which engaged Buddhists in stimulating debate.

Above Mahayana bhikkhus made long and dangerous journeys into the Himalayan kingdoms to spread the teachings. These young monks are learning the scriptures in Bumthang, Bhutan, in viharas that were founded during the 7th century CE.

As he responded to these challenges, Nagarjuna formulated ideas that furthered the development of Buddhist thought. He called himself a *sunyatavadin*, 'a person who holds to the position of emptiness'. His position on emptiness was to demonstrate through logic that no phenomenon has an eternal, fixed 'self-nature' (*svabhava*), or identity, and that it is precisely this emptiness (*sunyata*), this lack of a fixed identity, that enables change to take place – night to merge into day, life into death, ignorance into enlightenment. Change cannot bring itself about. There is no ultimate cause for anything that exists, and phenomena come into being not by their own volition

Left Nagarjuna's ideas on the emptiness of the physical and mental worlds were significant not just for Buddhism, but also for the evolution of philosophy. Generations of philosophers have studied his writings.

Right The goal of a bodhisattva is to attain the ability to see things in a non-dualistic way; to realize, for example, that good and bad are not entirely opposed. This is a higher perception of the world.

or power but by externally interacting conditions. He applied these arguments equally to nirvana, once famously stating that "there is, on the part of samsara, no difference at all from nirvana".

Nagarjuna asserted that reality is a mental construct, an illusion. To address such dualities, implicit in all thinking about *sunyata*, he posited a doctrine of 'two truths'. There is conventional truth, in the sense of apparent and measurable reality (for example, things and beings seem independent, possessed of an enduring self); and there is ultimate truth, in the sense of higher understandings (for example, the perception that everything lacks a core essence, or permanent selfhood). To understand this is to become aware of how our perception of the world is conditioned by assumptions and attitudes, and to liberate the mind from clinging to accepted truths.

THE MIDDLE WAY

After Nagarjuna's death a new school, the Madhyamaka, arose among commentators on his writings, particularly those on emptiness and his *Mulamadhyamakakarika*, or *Fundamental Verses on the Middle Way*. Followers of the Madhyamaka school adhere

Right Meditating monks who reached high trance states experienced the mind as pure and separate from worldly experience. This may have inspired the Yogacara idea that consciousness is the only reality.

Right The goal of a bodhisattva is to attain the ability to see things in a non-dualistic way; to realize, for example, that good and bad are not entirely opposed. This is a higher perception of the world.

to Nagarjuna's interpretations of reality. They see this position as midway between opposing views: the belief that phenomena, including human beings, possess a core eternal, unchanging self; and the Indian view of nihilism – the idea that all phenomena have been annihilated and cease to exist.

Madhyamakas believe that *sunyata* is not nihilism (in the ancient Indian or modern Western interpretation of the word). To grasp the interdependence of all phenomena is to abandon the dualistic view of the universe, good/bad, samsara/ nirvana, and to see things as they really are. This is a step on the way to enlightenment.

THE CONSCIOUSNESS SCHOOL

Around the 4th century CE, a new school emerged in India that took Nagarjuna's thinking in a different direction. Its name, Yogacara, stems from its emphasis on yoga and meditation, which its followers saw as the key to enlightenment. Yogacara sought to avoid nihilism and instead developed a philosophy known as *cittamatra*, or mind-only – the idea that the world of objects does not exist, and that consciousness is the only reality.

The Yogacara introduced a new concept that they called 'storehouse consciousness', in which the effects of willed actions are stored in the consciousness as seeds. These seeds take root and ultimately transform the individual's consciousness.

BUDDHISM CROSSES BORDERS

DURING THE FIRST MILLENIUM CE, BUDDHISM SPREAD NORTHWARD FROM INDIA TO CENTRAL ASIA. MONKS FROM INDIA'S GREAT SEATS OF LEARNING TOOK NEW BUDDHIST IDEAS INTO TIBET, AND BY 1000CE, BUDDHISM HAD BECOME AN INTERNATIONAL RELIGION.

Taxila, ancient India's respected centre of Vedic learning, was at the confluence of trade routes linking India with Kashmir, Bactria (Balkh) and Central Asia. People of all religions from across the known world enrolled to learn Sanskrit grammar, medicine, law, military science and ayurvedic medicine, as well as the Veda.

The first Buddhist monasteries were founded at Taxila during the 3rd century CE, and Buddhist monks, confronted by sceptical enquiry into their beliefs, participated in debates on religious issues. By about the 1st century CE, Mahayana viharas there had become famous for advances in logic and philosophical analysis.

Buddhism continued to develop in Taxila, even when its fortifications were overridden by waves of invaders – kings from Greece, Parthia (an Iranian empire) and, during the 2nd and 3rd centuries, the Kushan empire. During times of peace, monks carried Buddhism to centres along the trade routes, to Bactria, Samarkand – the capital of neighbouring Sogdiana – Parthia, Sassanid Persia, and even Merv (modern Mary, Turkmenistan).

THE EMPEROR KANISHKA

The Kushans were originally Yuezhi tribal people from the Mongolian steppe, and their empire, which was bordered by the Himalayas, extended from Central Asia to northern India. The mid-2nd-century Kushan emperor, Kanishka I, became a Buddhist and spread Buddhism into what is now Afghanistan, into Central Asia and thence to China. By the 7th century, Buddhism was flourishing in the oasis towns of the Tarim Basin.

Above A small tiered stupa stands in what was once a monk's cell at the Mohra Moradu vihara on the archaeological site of Taxila, Pakistan.

NALANDA

Before the 4th century CE, Chinese pilgrims were journeying to northern India in search of Buddhist scriptures for translation. Many texts were copied and translated into Sanskrit at Nalanda. Mahayana doctrine took shape at this seat of Buddhist learning, and its libraries became the main repository of Mahayana sutras. Students travelled from all over the Buddhist world to sit at the feet of its many outstanding teachers, such as renowned logician Dharmakirti, and Shantideva, a philosopher of the Madhyamaka school.

From Nalanda, monks spread Buddhism widely through China, from where it reached Korea and Japan, and to parts of Southeast Asia. By the 7th century, Nalanda had become a famous international Buddhist university.

Left The high passes of the Pamir Mountains were a through route for the spread of Buddhism into Central and East Asia and for merchants and scholars entering India from the Silk Route.

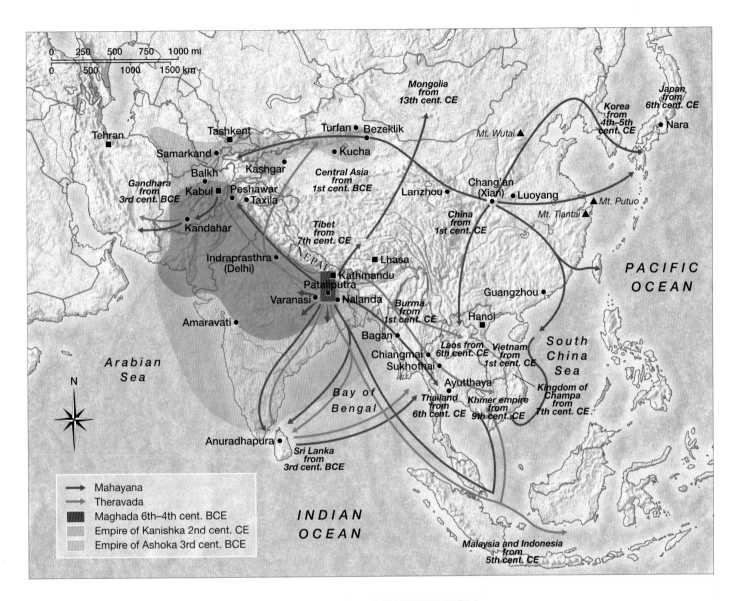

Map legend:
- → Mahayana
- → Theravada
- ■ Maghada 6th–4th cent. BCE
- Empire of Kanishka 2nd cent. CE
- Empire of Ashoka 3rd cent. BCE

Map labels:
0 250 500 750 1000 mi
0 500 1000 1500 km

Tehran • Tashkent • Turfan • Bezeklik
Mongolia from 13th cent. CE
Japan from 6th cent. CE
Korea from 4th–5th cent. CE
Nara
Mt. Wutai ▲
Samarkand • Kucha
Balkh Kashgar
Central Asia from 1st cent. BCE
Chang'an (Xian) • Luoyang
Gandhara from 3rd cent. BCE
Kabul ■ Peshawar • Taxila
Lanzhou
China from 1st cent. CE
Mt. Putuo
Mt. Tiantai ▲
Kandahar
Tibet from 7th cent. CE
Indraprasthra (Delhi)
Lhasa
NEPAL
Kathmandu
Pataliputra
PACIFIC OCEAN
Varanasi • Nalanda
Guangzhou
Amaravati •
Burma from 1st cent. CE
Hanoi
Arabian Sea
N
Bagan •
Chiangmai • Sukhothai
Laos from 6th cent. CE
Vietnam from 1st cent. CE
South China Sea
Ayutthaya
Thailand from 6th cent. CE
Khmer empire from 9th cent. CE
Kingdom of Champa from 7th cent. CE
Bay of Bengal
Anuradhapura •
Sri Lanka from 3rd cent. BCE
INDIAN OCEAN
Malaysia and Indonesia from 5th cent. CE

THE ORIGINS OF TIBETAN BUDDHISM

From the 10th century, Tibetans travelled to Nalanda, whose libraries held copies of the *Prajñaparamita,* or Perfection of Wisdom sutras, and many tantras. The university became the focus for the development of Vajrayana, a strand of Mahayana Buddhism based on belief in the potential buddhahood of every being, and on practices such as the recitation of mantras.

Vikramashila, a new university of advanced learning (in what is now Bihar), overtook Nalanda in size and reputation during the 10th century, and became the established centre in India for Tantric Buddhism. Students from

THE SPREAD OF BUDDHISM

This map shows the spread of Buddhism, from its roots in India across the Asian continent, between the 5th century BCE and the end of the 1st millennium CE.

Tibet and elsewhere flocked to study under famed teachers, such as Dipankara Srijnana, called Atisha. During the mid-11th century, Atisha travelled to Tibet, where he was instrumental in revivifying Buddhism, which was

at that time in decline there. He resided at the Samye monastery in central Tibet, where he translated texts from Sanskrit into Tibetan.

During the 12th century, Buddhism declined in India, but as the map above shows, it continued to spread northward and eastward during succeeding centuries.

Left The spread of Buddhism was encouraged by Emperor Kanishka, the 2nd century CE ruler of the Kushan empire, which extended from Central Asia to Afghanistan, where the remains of Buddhist temples, such as this one at Takht-i-Rustam, can still be seen.

TIBETAN BUDDHISM

TIBETAN BUDDHISM IS THE NAME BY WHICH THE WEST KNOWS THE NEW BUDDHIST TRADITION THAT EMERGED IN INDIA IN THE 7TH CENTURY CE, AND WHICH, BY THE END OF THE 1ST MILLENNIUM, WAS FLOURISHING IN TIBET AND SURROUNDING REGIONS.

The third major tradition of Buddhism emerged from the Mahayana in the 7th century CE. It was at first called Tantrayana ('Tantra Vehicle'), or Tantric Buddhism, because many of its beliefs and practices were based on scriptures called tantras. It was also known as Mantrayana ('Mantra Vehicle'), because the recitation of mantras – sacred words or sounds – was central to its practice. Tantric Buddhism is often described as 'esoteric', or 'secret', mainly because tantric techniques were open only to the initiated. To maintain secrecy, tantras were kept hidden and some were written in code.

Below Monks at the Jokhang temple in Lhasa chant tantras, marking their progress by ringing hand bells. Ritual practices such as these are important features of Tibetan Buddhist devotions.

A variation of the new tradition, which emerged during the 8th century CE, was Vajrayana. *Vajra* means 'diamond' and also 'thunderbolt' – Vajrayana saw the tantric way as cutting through and destroying ignorance and other fetters that tie beings to samsara. Vajrayana Buddhism originated from ideas of the Madhyamaka and the meditational focus of the 4th-century Yogacara school.

Both forms of Buddhism use techniques to enable devotees to reach enlightenment instantly. They use mantras and mandalas, for example, to deepen concentration, with the aim of accelerating the loss of self and so bringing about instant liberation and attainment of the state of buddhahood.

Because the new tradition spread northward, into Tibet, the surrounding Himalayan kingdoms,

Above Mani are rocks traditionally inscribed with the mantra Om mani padme hum ('Hail to the jewel in the heart of the lotus'). Mantras are sacred chants to clear the mind for meditation or to express devotion.

Mongolia and into parts of Russia, it is also known as Northern Buddhism.

TANTRIC TECHNIQUES
The Northern tradition may have begun as early as the 5th century CE in north-western and north-eastern India as part of a wider movement that also influenced Hinduism and Jainism with its

Below This Tibetan painting depicts Vajrasattva, Bodhisattva of the Diamond Light. His right hand holds a vajra ('diamond sceptre'), symbolizing the destruction of ignorance, against his heart.

Above Kalmyk followers of Tibetan Buddhism wait outside the Khurul Datsan (monastery) north-east of their capital, Elista, in the northern Caucasus, to greet the Dalai Lama during his 2004 visit to their region.

tantric techniques. These include meditation and yoga; the reciting of mantras; mysticism and mudras. As it spread, Buddhism adapted to local religions, absorbing popular beliefs in magic and ritual.

The *Guhya-samaja-tantra*, or 'Tantra of the Secret Society', an early text, introduces the idea of multiple buddhas – the five Dhyani Buddhas. Each may appear during trance meditation as one of five bodhisattvas. The Adi-buddha, or Primordial Buddha, who existed in time before anything else, is said to have given rise to the Dhyani Buddhas.

MANTRAS AND MANDALAS

All schools of Tibetan Buddhism emphasize reliance on a spiritual guru, who can transmit not only texts and teachings but also spiritual energy to the acolyte. All are strongly devotional – as well as prostrations, prayers and practices such as the recitation of mantras for spiritual purification, visualization techniques using mandalas are important.

A mandala is a sacred representation of the Buddhist universe. Through meditation, devotees visualize themselves entering the mandala, passing through its outer circles, which represent the

Above The Samye gompa *near Lhasa was Tibet's first Buddhist vihara, founded in the 8th century by Padmasambhava. It is designed as a sacred mandala, with a central temple symbolizing Mount Meru, the centre of the Buddhist universe.*

external world, and following the path through the gateways leading to the bodhisattva or buddha at the centre. They visualize losing their sense of self and actually becoming the deity. Chanting, ringing bells and other ritual practices, many of them esoteric, or secret, feature in devotions. They are believed to invoke the help of deities for protection from danger or ensure personal salvation.

By the 8th century CE, tantric techniques dominated Indian Buddhism. Their appeal for Mahayana monks was that they seemed an effective, even powerful medium for achieving enlightenment and buddhahood.

NEW DIRECTIONS

The tradition became established in Tibet after the 7th century CE, spreading from there to surrounding kingdoms and northward to Mongolia and eastward to China, Korea and Japan, where it still

flourishes as Shingon Buddhism. Intertwined with the beliefs of native religions, Tibetan Buddhism took tantrism in new directions, searching for meditation and other techniques that would lead to enlightenment in one lifetime.

Many centuries earlier, texts such as the *Guhyasamaja-tantra* had posited the gratification of desire as a path to liberation. Later, Tantric Buddhists developed this idea and sought to achieve transcendence of the self through techniques involving ritual sexual intercourse.

Tibetan Buddhism continues to evolve. Suppressed in its homeland, it has migrated to the West, where it has flourished.

TIBETAN SCRIPTURES

ALL THE EXTRAVAGANT COMPLEXITY OF TIBETAN BUDDHISM — THE RICH COSMOLOGY AND SYMBOLISM, DEITIES AND DEMONS, MANDALAS, MANTRAS AND MYSTICISM — CAN BE FOUND IN THE SUTRAS AND TANTRAS ON WHICH IT IS BASED.

Tantric beliefs and practices were first transmitted by word of mouth before the 5th century CE, when tantras were first written down by monks who may have wanted to revive spirituality in Buddhism at a time when it had become dry and academic. Tantras appeared up to the 12th century, by which time, Buddhism had almost disappeared from India, though it was flourishing in the surrounding regions where it had spread.

Above Sacred texts, or tantras, were written in a script that was specially devised for them, and were sometimes embellished with inks made from precious metals and stones.

THE TIBETAN COLLECTIONS

Tibetan Buddhism's sacred scriptures form two major collections. The *Kanjur* (Translated Word of the Buddha) consists of 108 volumes and more than 1,000 texts of the Buddha's teachings. The *Tenjur* (Treatises) contains more than 3,000 commentaries on the *Kanjur* texts in 225 volumes, plus poems and songs of praise, manuals on meditation and mandalas, rituals for consecrating monasteries and commentaries on doctrine.

Most of the texts of the *Kanjur* and *Tenjur* were written in Indian languages and were subsequently translated into Tibetan. No Tibetan script existed until the 7th century, when a king, Songtsen Gampo, instructed a learned courtier to devise one so that the Dharma could be translated from Sanskrit and read to his people. The period of feverish translation that followed ensured the preservation in Tibetan of Sanskrit texts that might have been lost. The work of identifying, classifying, recording and translating this voluminous literature still continues today.

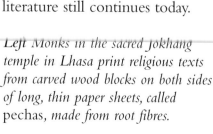

Left Monks in the sacred Jokhang temple in Lhasa print religious texts from carved wood blocks on both sides of long, thin paper sheets, called pechas, *made from root fibres.*

THE TANTRAS

The sutras and tantras of Tibetan Buddhism purport to be the word of the Buddha, which was kept secret for centuries until Buddhists were ready to understand the texts. Thus, the arcane and esoteric nature of much of Tibetan Buddhism stems directly from its scriptures. There are some 450 tantras in the *Kanjur* and more than 2,400 in the *Tenjur*. These deal with the esoteric aspects of Buddhist teaching – tantra originally meant 'loom' or 'weaving' and symbolized the harmony of body and mind – but it later became associated with occult teachings. Many tantras were written in a 'twilight language' or *Sandhabhasya* so that only an initiate – a lama (or guru) – could read them and impart the teachings to selected students.

The tantras are classified into four or five major groups. The largest and earliest is the Kriya group, written between the 5th and 7th centuries. It is concerned with cultivating the magical powers of mantras and meditation to achieve worldly goals such as control of illness and weather.

Later groups were concerned with achieving buddhahood – but not gradually, over many disciplined lives. They sought instant transformation into buddhas. The most important of the eight Carya tantras focuses on identification with the Buddha Vairocana, a symbol of ultimate reality, while the principal Yoga tantra of the 8th century centres on Mañjushri, who symbolized wisdom.

Ritual sexual practices featured in the later tantras – the male symbolizing compassionate action

Right A lama studies the Tibetan scriptures. Lamas ministering to a dead or dying person recite passages from the Bardo Thodrol.

Above An image of the revered Tibetan yogin Milarepa (1040–1123) carved into rock. Milarepa is most famous for his poems, The Hundred Thousand Songs of Milarepa, *in which he extols the Dharma. These poems are part of the Tibetan canon.*

and the female wisdom – as did the consumption of forbidden substances, such as alcohol and meat. One objective of such practices was to liberate the mind from dualistic thinking (bad/good). A result of this phase of Tantric Buddhism was the importance attributed to female bodhisattvas. Female deities figure prominently in 9th–10th-century Yogini tantras.

THE TIBETAN BOOK OF THE DEAD

The *Bardo Thodrol*, known in English as *The Tibetan Book of the Dead*, is a scripture on the theme of death, life after death and rebirth. It describes the world called 'Bardo' that lies between death and rebirth.

One of the duties of Tibetan lamas is to read 'The Great Liberation by Hearing' from the *Bardo Thodrol* to the dying. This is part of the rite of passage for the dying person.

The work is a spiritual treasure that Padmasambhava, the sage said to have brought Tantric Buddhism to Tibet, is believed to have hidden in the wilds of the Himalayas. It was later found by the Tibetan religious *terton*, or 'treasure hunter', Karma Lingpa.

The Tibetan Book of the Dead has been lauded as a great contribution to world literature on the states of dying and death, but Padmasambhava offers wise guidance on transforming everyday living, as well as addressing one's own experience of dying and how to help dying people.

INDEX